Miracle in Motion

by
Tim Storey

Miracle in Motion

by
Tim Storey

Vincom, Inc.
Tulsa, Oklahoma

Unless otherwise indicated, all Scripture quotations are taken from the *King James Version* of the Bible.

Miracle in Motion
ISBN 0-927936-33-X
Copyright ©1992 by Tim Storey
P. O. Box 1428
Whittier, CA 90609

Published by Vincom, Inc.
P. O. Box 702400
Tulsa, OK 74170
(918) 254-1276

Contents

Contents

1

Faith To Change Your World

Most of us tend to believe that the big moves in the Church, the ones that literally changed the world, were accomplished by extraordinary people. We tend to believe that God chose the "heroes and heroines" of faith (Heb. 11) because they were *special* in some way.

However, if Christians truly catch hold of the revelation that the greatest moves of God have come through *ordinary* people, the Church of today will be different. All Christians have the necessary faith available to change their worlds — if only they will believe it, exercise it, and walk in it.

Can you imagine what would happen if enough of us began to grasp the purpose and plan of God for us and our world? Can you imagine what God could do in our families, our jobs, our churches, our cities, and our world?

Abraham, Isaac, and Jacob were *ordinary* men called to accomplish *extraordinary* feats for God. Moses was an ordinary man. James wrote that Elijah was an *ordinary* man.

> ...The effectual fervent prayer of a righteous man availeth much.
>
> Elias (Elijah) was a man subject to like passions as we are, and he prayed earnestly that it might not

rain: and it rained not on the earth by the space of three years and six months.

And he prayed again, and the heaven gave rain, and the earth brought forth her fruit.

James 5:16-18

James was telling the Christians of his day something that is true for any century. All Christians are *ordinary* people, plagued with the same flesh and soul problems. But *an effectual, fervent prayer* can make a way for God to bring about earth-shaking events.

In terms of sovereignty and power, God can do what He pleases, whether we do anything or not. However, *He* set up the rules over this earth which determined mankind would have dominion (Gen. 1:28), so He does very few things without moving on some man or woman to cooperate with Him in one way or another.

Most of us know that the dominion, or the rule, over the earth was forfeited by Adam and Eve to Satan. But Jesus defeated Satan on the cross (Col. 2:14,15; 1 John 3:8), and dominion over the earth reverted back to Christ, who delegated it to us as His Body.

John Wesley, founder of Methodism and instrumental in the Great Awakening in the mid-eighteenth century, said that God does nothing on earth unless somebody prays. In that statement, the phrase *in faith* is understood. The Bible makes clear that prayers without faith expressed in action are *ineffectual*. That means they are not "working" prayers but simply words.

If Elijah was just like us, and all of those other heroes and heroines were just like us, then what enabled them to do all of the extraordinary things we are told about in the Word of God?

The thing that made the difference was *faith in God*. Their belief that God existed, that all of the things handed down through their forefathers and told to them about the Almighty were true, enabled them to develop a faith that changed their worlds.

All of them began with "a measure of faith" and, by obedience to everything God told them and seeing the results of small steps of faith, they moved on to great leaps of faith. *We can do the same!*

We may live in a post-Christian society, but most of us still remember the truths about God that we were taught at home, in church, and even for some of us, in school. All of the heroes and heroines of faith lived surrounded by a pagan society. Elijah lived in the northern kingdom of Israel in a time when that ten-tribed nation was a "post-Israelite" society.

The rulers of Israel, from the beginning of the divided kingdoms of Israel and Judah, had initiated a gradual move toward the worship of false gods and demons. By Elijah's day, the whole country was permeated by idolatry. Read the book of Amos as it describes Israel from about Elijah's time to its being swept away by Assyria. You could very easily think Amos was speaking to the United States of America.

Once again, we need to pray fervently for God to raise up some ordinary people to do extraordinary things. I want to be one of those people. Would you like to be used of God that way? After you read this book, I believe you will have a clearer revelation that you can do great exploits for God — whether it is through intercession or working in the ministry.

Your "great exploit" may be praying for others. Intercessors are on the front lines, spiritually speaking, although they may never be recognized in the natural. Without extraordinary things being done in prayer, none of the moves of God would have occurred as James told us with his comment about Elijah. God honored Elijah's prayer of faith when He withheld the rain and then restored it. It is also assumed in James' statement that Elijah prayed in the *will* of God.

If you find the will of God in a situation and then pray fervently for that thing to be done, it *will* happen.

I want to give you an example from our own times of an ordinary man who was the instrument for one of the most extraordinary restorations of God's power to the Church in the past two thousand years.

Most Christians have heard of the Azusa Street revival in which people from more than fifty nations came to Los Angeles to be touched by the power of God. This restoration of the gifts of the Holy Spirit to the Body of Christ set the tone for everything else God has done in the 20th century.

What happened there was equal to any of the great exploits of the heroes of the Bible. It was like the early days of the Church when Peter, Paul, and the other apostles were turning their world upside down. (Acts 17:6.) Azusa Street literally turned the modern Church world upside down. Until we reach Heaven, we will not know all of the ramifications or the far-reaching implications of Azusa Street.

Revival on Azusa Street

Anyone who has heard of this revival probably has heard more about a white man named Charles F. Parham, whose Bible school in Kansas and later in Houston, Texas, is considered the "spiritual soil" in which the seeds for Azusa Street were sown. However, fewer people have heard of a black, one-eyed man named William J. Seymour who took the few seeds he received from Parham and ran with them to accomplish a mighty move of God.

Recently, the Lord moved on me to develop a video about this revival, a documentary, which I believe, is the only one of its kind. During the making of that video, I not only did a lot of study and research on the times and the move of God, but I interviewed the only person still living who is known to have been there. My own faith to do great things for God was increased through a firsthand look at this move of God through ordinary people.

From a Bible study in Texas, the next step God directed in the progress toward Azusa Street was to lead William Seymour to California where a small prayer meeting had been started in the home of a janitor and his wife. The address is not as well-known as Azusa Street, but without the "ordinary" prayer meeting at 214 (now 216) Bonnie Brae Street, the rest would not have happened.

In a later chapter, I want to show you that God moves one step at a time, and we need to do the same. It may look as if something suddenly exploded into being, but if you could trace the events leading up to that revival, move, or great ministry, you would see that one "stone" was placed on another.

So without Richard and Ruth Asberry, who owned that house on Bonnie Brae Street — or without someone like them — the next step toward God's move would not have happened. Also, I think God delights in this kind of thing, because the enemy has no idea what is going on until it explodes. The prayer meeting and Bible study of a small group of black people certainly was nothing to attract the notice of the enemy.

It was no different in the natural than many such meetings going on all over the country.

"Azusa" first happened on Bonnie Brae Street where there was another ordinary person to whom God gave an opportunity to become involved in His plan. Mrs. Julia Hutchins, along with eight other families, had been expelled from the Second Baptist Church for teaching holiness. After the Lord joined her group with the Asberrys, the meetings grew so much that they had to open a storefront mission, which was on Santa Fe Street.[1]

Early in 1906, the Lord began to connect the various people whom He had called to participate in this move. A young woman from Hutchins' mission had visited a church in Houston where Seymour was pastoring. She invited him to come to Los Angeles with the possibility of becoming pastor, and he was called. His first service was held on February 22, 1906.

Part of the transformation of Seymour from an ordinary man to one who did extraordinary things was the boldness in him concerning the "new" message of the baptism of the Holy Spirit. What is even more exciting is that, although he totally believed in the baptism for today and preached it against all obstacles, he had not yet received it! That is almost the equivalent of someone preaching Jesus as the way to salvation when he has not yet been saved. Yet, that is what Seymour did, and many were baptized in the Holy Spirit through his preaching before he was.

He preached on Acts 2:4 on his very first Sunday and insisted that speaking in tongues was the evidence of the baptism, which was contrary to the holiness doctrine. Holiness adherents believed you could be filled with the Spirit but not speak in tongues. The result was that Mrs. Hutchins locked the church door against him.

From this we can see that some ordinary people called by God do not always obey the call. Many are called, but few are chosen (Matt. 20:16), because the majority usually refuse the call. I suspect that many people have missed the opportunity to do great exploits by allowing doctrines and traditions to block them from receiving direction from God.

Certain people in the Bible are called "heroes and heroines" *because* they believed God, and it was counted to them for righteousness — not because of their great exploits. We will never know how many others God called, who either did not respond or who actively blocked what He was doing thinking they were "defending the faith."

Seymour continued to live with Mr. and Mrs. Edward Lee, who allowed him to hold Bible studies in their home. Within a few days, the group grew too large for the Lee home. Guess who took Seymour in after that? The "ordinary" janitor and his wife, the Asberrys. God backed up behind Mrs. Hutchins to the ones who had first been obedient and gave them a second opportunity, which they also took.

The Lees, like so many of those God used as connecting threads in this tapestry He was weaving around the ministry of the Holy Spirit, are not very well-known in our day. However, they had significant roles that are known in Heaven. In addition to making a way for Seymour to remain in Los Angeles and preach, Lee became the first person there to receive the baptism of the Spirit with the evidence of speaking in tongues.

April 9, 1906, should be a "red-letter" day in the annals of Pentecostalism. That was the day Lee called Seymour at 6 p.m. and requested prayer to receive the baptism. Over the past five or six weeks of Bible study and prayer meetings, Lee had come to believe wholeheartedly in Seymour's message.

Lee asked Seymour to pray for him for healing, but he received an additional blessing: Immediately he was filled with the Spirit and began to speak in tongues. From praying over Lee, Seymour went directly to Bonnie Brae Street to begin the evening service. Again, he spoke on Acts 2:4 and told the group about Lee's breakthrough. Reports are that he never finished the teaching that evening. Someone else immediately began to speak in tongues, then others and others.

One of those others was a woman named Jennie Evans Moore. She owned the house across the street from the Asberrys. At the Asberry home, there was a piano but no one knew how to play. When Jennie was filled with the Spirit, she moved to the piano and began to play melodies and sing in various languages.

According to church historians, six different languages came forth through Jennie Moore during her lifetime. They were a Hindu dialect, Spanish, Latin, French, Hebrew, and Greek. She was a black woman, who had never studied languages and had never learned to play the piano — another "ordinary" person used in a spectacular way by God.

The Beginning of the Extraordinary

For several weeks, Seymour had preached at the Asberry home, and the crowds had grown so significantly that he had to preach from the front porch on Bonnie Brae Street. Three days after the Lee/Evans incident, so many people came that the front porch collapsed. Another place had to be found for the meetings.

At this point, word of the outbreak of Pentecostalism traveled through the black community and on into the white community, and as a result, the real crowds that marked this revival began to gather.

Seymour held the first meetings on Azusa Street on April 14, 1906. They had found an old barn of a building that once had been the Stevens African Methodist Episcopal Church, then a warehouse for a large department store chain, and finally a livery stable.

By this time, the devil must have known something was happening, and if he did not, he knew it by April 18. That was the day of the great San Francisco earthquake, and the very same day, newspaper headlines in Los Angeles carried the first story of "weird" happenings at the mission where more than a thousand people were trying to get into the 40-by-60 foot building.

Again, until we get the full story from the Lord Himself, we will never know what ordinary people God used to pray through for the move so that the quake was not able to move on down the fault lines to Los Angeles. Also, San Francisco was a very wicked city at the time, much as it is today. Anything went — from gambling to white slavery, to say nothing of all of the "ordinary" crimes — and it was called "the Barbary Coast."

Or perhaps the quake was a spiritual response to what was breaking forth in Los Angeles, a literal pulling down of strongholds of the enemy through the emerging prayers in tongues at a second "Day of Pentecost." On the first Day of Pentecost, a "spiritual earthquake'' occurred in Jerusalem, and thousands were saved eventually affecting billions of people.

On this second Day of Pentecost — April 14, 1906 — we know for sure that more than half a billion people have been affected as a result with no telling how many more by the time the Lord returns.

Most Christians do not know the meaning of the word *Azusa*. It was the name of an ancient Shoshone Indian village located on that site, and it means *blessed miracle*.[2] Think how far ahead God knew what was going to happen at that location and how He caused a then-pagan people to prophetically name the place for His purpose.

In the next chapter, I want to take a closer look at two Bible heroes and at William Seymour, a hero of our own times. I want to show you how God moved these three step by step to their destinies in Him. And I want you to see that, *if He could do it with them, He can do it with you.*

Notes

[1]Burgess, Stanley M. and McGee, Gary B. *Dictionary of Pentecostal and Charismatic Movements*, ''Azusa Street Revival,'' (Grand Rapids: Regency Reference Library, Zondervan Publishing House, 1988), pp. 31-36.

[2]*God's Glorious Outpouring: The Azusa Street Revival* (Whittier: CTL Productions, Inc., 1992). Video available from Tim Storey Ministries.

2

People Whose Faith Changed Their Worlds

The Azusa Street revival was the beginning of what we know as the Pentecostal movement, out of which came the Healing revival of the 1940s and 1950s, the Charismatic movement of the 1960s on, and even the smaller Word of Faith movement. The Azusa Street revival, which William Seymour was used to start, will be the basis for much else God does in this century. Its impact will never be totally understood in the natural realm.

I have said that Spike Lee is not my hero, Malcolm X is not my hero, Bill Cosby is not my hero. If we are looking for black heroes, we have found one, and his name is *William Seymour*. But before we take a closer look at him, let us look at two people in the Bible — a man and a woman — whose lives mirror the same kind of principles and patterns that Seymour's did thousands of years later.

The first one is Deborah, one of the judges of Israel, and the second is Elijah, a prophet to kings. Both played extraordinary roles in national affairs of their times, as well as in spiritual matters.

The book of Judges covers a period in Israel's history between the taking of the Promised Land and the time when the people demanded a king over them. During the period of judges, the Bible says that most of the time the people decided things for themselves.

> **In those days there was no king in Israel, but every man did that which was right in his own sight.**

> **And the children of Israel departed thence at that time, every man to his tribe and to his family, and they went out from thence every man to his inheritance.**

> **In those days there was no king in Israel: every man did that which was right in his own eyes.**
>
> **Judges 17:6; 21:24,25**

However, in times of national emergencies, God raised up a man or a woman to lead the nation.

> **Nevertheless the Lord raised up judges, which delivered them out of the hand of those that spoiled them.**
>
> **Judges 2:16**

Deborah was the fourth of the twelve judges, and the only woman among them. In Hebrew, her name means "a bee." God used her as a busy little bee to help a man named Barak, a fearful person, become the man of God he was supposed to be. His name in Hebrew means "lightning," but he did not start out that way.

This prophetess-judge was the ordinary wife of a man named Lapidoth and lived under a palm tree on Mount Ephraim. All Israel came up to her for judgment. That means she settled the problems and conflicts people could not handle themselves.

The Bible does not tell us much about her background, but we can gather some things from what we are told. The Israelites had again fallen into evil in the sight of the Lord after the third judge, Ehud, died. Therefore, the Lord "sold them into the hand" of the

Canaanites, whose top general was a man named Sisera. The Israelites cried out to God after, and probably also during, the twenty years of this oppression. (Judg. 4:1-3.)

> And she (Deborah) sent and called Barak the son of Abinoam out of Kedesh-naphtali, and said unto him, Hath not the Lord God of Israel commanded, saying, Go and draw toward mount Tabor, and take with thee ten thousand men of the children of Naphtali and of the children of Zebulun?
>
> And I will draw unto thee to the river Kishon Sisera, the captain of Jabin's army, with his chariots and his multitude; and I will deliver him into thine hand.
>
> **Judges 4:6,7**

Barak had a good reason to be somewhat uneasy about going into battle. Sisera had nine hundred chariots of iron. (Judg. 4:3.) At that time, Israel had no chariots of iron. So Barak told Deborah he would go but only if she went with him. Then she told him that little bit of self-will — of setting the conditions under which he would obey God — would cost him the honor of the victory. God was going to give Sisera into the hand of a woman.

> . . . And Deborah arose, and went with Barak to Kedesh.
>
> And Deborah said unto Barak, Up; for this is the day in which the Lord hath delivered Sisera into thine hand: is not the Lord gone out before thee? . . . .
>
> And the Lord discomfited Sisera, and all of his chariots, and all his host, with the edge of the sword before Barak; so that Sisera lighted down off his chariot, and fled away on his feet.
>
> **Judges 4:9,14,15**

The rest of the story is that the Canaanite general ran to a tent in a community of Kenites, who had not been driven out of the Promised Land by Israel but who were at peace with the Canaanites. Sisera sought refuge in a Kenite tent where a woman named Jael lived. She gave the hard-pressed general some milk and a place to lie down and rest.

However, when he was asleep, she took a hammer and nail and drove the nail through his temple into the ground. Barak, following Sisera's trail, soon arrived at the tent to find that, just as Deborah had prophesied, the praise for the victory went to Jael, not himself.

We notice from the story several things about Deborah:

• Firstly, she had a word from God, and obviously, in order to hear, she had an intimate knowledge of the Lord that made her faith strong. She heard Him and *believed* Him.

• Secondly, she was a strong woman, even ready to go to war if that was necessary to carry out the will of God.

• The third thing is that Deborah was willing to go the extra mile.

When faith truly works in your life, you can believe for things in other people's lives. She had given the Lord's word to Barak, but he refused to go alone. She was like the mailman with a letter for Barak, which he refused to accept. At that point, the "mailman's" job is over.

She could have walked off, saying, "Okay, Lord. What do we do now? Who is your second choice?"

But this woman was so full of faith that she decided to see things from a God's-eye view. God sees those things that are not yet in existence as if they already are. (Rom. 4:17.) Of course, she was not "flaky" nor into unreality. She also saw things as they were. Barak, whose name meant "lightning" actually was living like lead, and she could have given up right then.

Instead, she chose to see things, like God, as they could be. God's men and women, who are true followers, usually choose to see things the way God does. However, that does not mean they do not see the reality of the natural realm. It simply means they understand the natural is temporary and subject to change and that true reality is what God sees. Jesus did the same thing. He called Peter a rock when he really was still a reed. The angel of the Lord called Gideon, who would be the next judge after Deborah, a "mighty man of valor" (Judg. 6:12), while Gideon was hiding from the Midianites in a wine press.

When Deborah talked to Barak that day, she had history in her hands. Because she went the second mile, Barak ended up in the "Hall of Fame of Faith-Heroes" — Hebrews 11. When he is first shown to us, he is nervous, however. He had "dead" faith and was going nowhere in a hurry.

Deborah could have left him there, and he would never have been anything in life. Be like Deborah and realize that you have history in your hands where your husband, child, or perhaps other people around you are concerned. Be ready to keep them company and give them courage as they go out to meet the enemy.

• Fourthly, Deborah saw the potential and not the problem. She saw what Barak could do, because she knew God would not have called him if he could not accomplish the task. She knew and focused on his potential and not on the problem of what to do if he did not make it, or the problem of his cowardice.

Her faith was developed in steps: faith for a word, faith *in* the word, putting action to her faith, and following through for the result. Now, let's take a look at Elijah.

Elijah the Tishbite

We do not know very much about Elijah's early life, even less than we know about Elisha's. The first time he is mentioned is in 1 Kings 17:1, where God sent him to give a word to Ahab about the rain. However, James told us a little more. He said Elijah *prayed*, and there was no rain for three and a half years.

When God withheld the rain, he sent Elijah somewhere to be looked after during the famine. First Elijah went to the brook Cherith, where ravens fed him twice a day, and he had good, clear water to drink. After a while, however, that brook dried up, and God gave Elijah the next part of the plan: Go to Zarephath and find a widow.

Here you can see the same pattern: Faith for a word from God, faith *in* the word, and putting action to faith. He *went* to Zarephath and found a widow gathering sticks to build a little fire, cook a little cake, eat it with her son, and then die. (1 Kings 17:12.)

I call these patterns "miracles in motion." Or, to repeat a saying I have been using for a long time: "Inch by inch, everything is a cinch!"

Faith means movement. Faith is never static. Elijah had faith in God, and he acted on that. The widow woman began with faith in the prophet, but after he raised her son from the dead, she said, "Now, I know you are a man of God." (1 Kings 17:24.) She developed faith in God.

From being ready to die, she became a blessing to her family, because she walked in faith. Faith for your miracle is birthed in your spirit, but you must keep the soulish nature quiet and patiently wait for the manifestation.

Elijah had a revelation, but he had to be patient and take the right steps of obedience in order for the miracle to manifest itself. A lot of people get weary in well-doing and stop before they reap their reward. The Greek word translated *weary* in Galatians 6:7 actually means "to have lost heart." A lot of people lose heart before their miracles manifest.

Look at the progression of God's dealings with Elijah:

• God spoke to Elijah about a famine; the famine occurred.

• God commanded ravens to feed him; the ravens fed him.

• The brook dried up; God commanded him to get up.

• Elijah rose up prepared to go wherever God said to go next.

You see this all the way through Elijah's life. I believe it was this progress that enabled him to come against the prophets of Baal.

Little successes or results convince your mind (which means the negative beliefs you have developed over the years) that God will give you the strength to tackle the big mountains in life. You cannot tackle mountains, however, until you learn to handle molehills.

I like a little story Fred Price, pastor/founder of Crenshaw Christian Center in Los Angeles, tells:

Suppose there was a guy in a restaurant who collapsed, and you came up to him and asked what was the matter.

He says, "I have not eaten for days, and I am starving."

And you say, "Do you *believe* that if you eat this food you will live?"

And he says, "Yes, I do believe it."

But you never give him food, or he never eats it, so he dies. Why? He *believed*, did he not? He died because faith without works is dead. (James 2:20,26.) Faith means action. There is no such thing as "passive" faith.

So Elijah got up from the brook and went to Zarephath. Notice that God did not tell him *which* widow it was. So how did he know? Most Bible scholars believe that he did not have a word of knowledge, but that he saw a poor woman gathering sticks and thought, "She could be the one."

He set out to test the promise by asking her for a drink of water. Then he asked her for the food. Again, it is a progression. It was no problem for her to give him the water. But, when he asked for food, she told him there was only enough for her and her son. She never mentioned a husband.

Elijah knew in his spirit by this time that this woman was the one. There were five steps Elijah took:

• He sat in faith as God instructed him concerning His will.

• He stood in faith on God's promises.

• He walked out the principles of God in his life in faith.

- He ran in faith.

- He soared in faith.

You can never get to the soaring stage in any area of your life unless you move through the progression of these other steps. You sit as a disciple of Jesus in some local church and are taught the Word. Then you stand on the promises, and also walk out the principles. That means the Word of God is in your life. As you follow this pattern of developing faith, you not only believe but you *know* the Word of God is true. After that, you get to the place where you can run and even soar to great heights of faith.

Another thing we can learn from Deborah and Elijah is that to be a great hero or heroine of faith, you have to go over some obstacles. The path is almost never easy. William Seymour certainly found that out. Another aspect of Seymour's life is that he was *hungry* for more of God, almost desperate for a closer spiritual walk.

Spiritual Hunger Brings Revival

Unfortunately, human nature often has to be desperate for help or God before people will move into that place of faith where He can really use them. God uses desperate people, who will in that desperation move toward Him.

Israel was desperate every time God appointed a judge or prophet to help them. If you are going to be a great person of faith, you must get to the place of desperation so that nothing counts but knowing more about God, and you must be prepared to overcome obstacles. All of the problems or obstacles that cross your path can be used as "weight-lifting" exercises to develop faith, when you trust God in the midst of them.

William Joseph Seymour had not one but several obstacles to overcome. He was black in a "Jim Crow" society. Not only that, he was a Christian and a pastor who was segregated from being able to participate in the meetings he needed to attend to keep moving in God. Also, he was blind in one eye from having smallpox as a young man, and he was poor and uneducated, earning his living as a waiter.

Even beyond that, he had to overcome the conditioning he received in fear of man, particularly toward whites, since his parents were Louisiana slaves. Born in 1870, shortly after the close of the Civil War, the black environment in which he grew up was not yet totally liberated from a slave-mentality or the fear of being oneself.

Seymour was called to preach while recovering from smallpox, pastored a church in Ohio, and then moved to Houston in search of his family.[1] There we begin to see God put "threads" together in preparation for Azusa Street. Seymour's *miracle* started to go into motion.

In 1903, Charles F. Parham hired a governess from Houston, Pastor Lucy Farrow, for his children while he was still operating the Bible school in Topeka. His 1900 class is the one that studied the baptism of the Holy Spirit and came to believe tongues were for today.

Guess who was chosen to follow Pastor Farrow in the pulpit of her Holiness church? Right! William Joseph Seymour. A couple of years later, Lucy Farrow returned to Houston demonstrating her new experience: speaking in tongues. Very soon afterwards,

Parham moved his Bible school to Houston, because of the persecution he had received in the Kansas area.

Seymour reached out at that time to overcome another obstacle, in the process taking another step in God's progression toward Azusa Street. He was *hungry* for all of the Lord he could get, so — in spite of segregation laws — he enrolled in Parham's school.

To satisfy the laws of the time, he could not sit in the class with the white students. However, it was arranged for him to sit outside the class in a hall where he could hear through the door. That meant he not only overcame the natural obstacle of segregation in order to learn about God, he had to overcome the flesh as well. He must have had to overcome pride or shame at being shut out. He had to make a conscious choice to be humble. He had to want God more than he minded being humiliated.

He reminds me of the Syrophenician woman who was so hungry for her daughter's healing that she persisted even when Jesus commented that "dogs should not eat from their masters' tables." (Mark 7:26-30.)

Many think that was a harsh thing for the Lord to say. However, He knew her heart, and He knew if her faith in Him could overcome the obstacle of pride, shame, or humiliation, she would receive what she came for. Jews of Jesus' day called all Gentiles "dogs," and the woman knew the play on words Jesus was making. (She knew that He was not calling *her* a dog.)

Seymour knew the Holy Spirit was saying, "Son, you are counted as a dog in this society, and you know it. Are you willing to sit outside the door and glean the crumbs from the white folks' table? Are you hungry enough for more of Me to ignore the humiliation?"

Obviously, Seymour was that hungry. He heard Parham's teachings and received the revelation from the Holy Spirit that the teachings were true. Tongues were for today. About this time, the young woman from Julia Hutchins church in Los Angeles visited Houston and came to Seymour's church. She invited him to come to Los Angeles to pursue the possibility of becoming pastor — and the rest is history.

William Seymour never lost his humility even when the crowds attending his Azusa Street Mission grew and grew, spilled out across the nation and, finally, exploded to the world. The Holy Spirit turned the tables, if Seymour had wanted to have a revengeful attitude. Whites began to attend his meetings in droves, but instead of demanding "an eye for an eye," Seymour graciously welcomed them. Azusa Street's "colored mission" became probably the first integrated church in America.

The mission always had a predominantly black congregation; however, whites held many leadership positions. Another innovation was the number of women who moved into leadership roles.

Seymour wanted so badly not to take any of the glory or credit that when the power of God fell, he often put a shoe crate over his head. He wanted so much to do the right thing that he wrote Parham in the summer of the outbreak attempting to get pastoral credentials under him.

He was ready to submit to Parham and recognize him as the true head of this revival that already had exploded. He had received the teachings on the baptism of the Holy Spirit from Parham, so he humbly prepared to receive Parham as his "spiritual father."

However, when Parham arrived in October of 1906, to hold a "union" revival of pulling together a number of churches, he was unable to make the next step in God's progression toward worldwide revival. He could not get past his traditions and beliefs to accept the noisy services, the integrated racial audience, some of the theology, and some of the other phenomena that characterized the revival. As a result, Parham was never really a part of Azusa Street.

Seymour was never ordained as part of Parham's Apostolic Faith movement, and the next year Parham was arrested on a morals charge that was dropped ultimately. Many say the incident was deliberately set up by those who would discredit him. Nevertheless, Parham's ministry never again was significant, and he died in 1929, an obscure figure to most of the Pentecostals of his day.

Everyone who attended Azusa Street had to overcome obstacles:

• Whites had to overcome prejudice and accept not only blacks as brothers and sisters in the congregation, but they had to accept that God had set a black man over this major, tremendously important move.

• Blacks had to overcome resentment and pride to sit with whites.

• All had to overcome traditional thinking about church services to receive the unstructured meetings that occurred. There was very little preaching, with meetings mostly characterized by testimonies, Bible studies — Seymour was more of a teacher than a preacher — praise and worship, and God sovereignly moving.

People were healed, baptized in the Spirit, delivered, and many miracles occurred — all through the sovereignty of the Holy Spirit. Only God could get the glory.

• All had to overcome "theology" to receive the teaching that the evidence of the baptism of the Holy Spirit was speaking in tongues. The Holiness movement which preceded Azusa Street and the Methodist movement before that stressed the baptism as "a second work of grace," following conversion and water baptism. But the emphasis of those movements was on "sanctification," the increased maturity and power of prayer that the baptism brought. What became the Pentecostal movement stressed the gifts of the Spirit.

• Everyone who attended had to endure being laughed at by the secular press, the world, and even some church people. The *Los Angeles Times* wrote of the "wild scenes" at the mission and called the services "a weird babble of tongues."[2]

• Everyone who came had to overcome the physical discomforts. Just as Jesus was born in a stable with animals and all of the unpleasant odors, bugs, and so forth that goes with stables, so Azusa Street was also born in what had at one time been used as a stable. The discomforts must have been pretty bad.

The benches were wooden; sawdust was on the floors; and flies laid eggs under the boards. When those eggs hatched that summer, flies were everywhere! In addition, air-conditioning had not been invented. Temperatures were over one hundred degrees — and still people would not leave. At times during the summer, the temperature was one hundred and ten degrees.

The building could hold a maximum of eight hundred people, and that was jam-packed. At times, several hundred more would be outside trying to hear. Sometimes they smashed out the windows so those outside could see and hear. Then, when a storm came, they would have to board up the windows.

I want you to see that another thing involved in *faith to change your world* is "choice" or "decision." Faith is not a rational (based on natural things) decision; it is not a mundane, everyday decision. Faith does not emerge from the soul (mind, will, and emotions). Faith is a strong decision made by the spirit man, the real you.

What is faith? Here are some answers my congregation gave: Faith is total trust in God, believing something Biblical against reason, and an action. The Bible says faith is the *substance* (in the Hebrew that means "title deed") of things not seen. (Heb. 11:1.)

Too many people today are having trouble in believing the promises God has given us. I suggest that they listen too much to what the soul believes and not to what the spirit man is receiving from the Holy Spirit. That means they are "double-minded." James wrote that being double-minded means being unstable in *all* your ways. He said a double-minded man will receive nothing from God. (James 1:8.)

Some of God's directions do not make sense to the soulish realm, such as walking around Jericho seven days blowing horns. But it worked. Tithing does not make sense to the soul, but try it — it works. God's instructions always usher in the desired results when we respond to them in *faith and obedience*.

Suppose Deborah, Elijah, and even William Seymour had made decisions based on what their minds thought or believed. Probably none of them would have been used by God to change their worlds. They would have been walking by sight, not faith. And we would not be able to see the results of their decisions.

The result of Deborah's and Elijah's faith decisions are written in the Word of God, but in the next chapter, I want to show you some results of Seymour's faith decisions.

Notes

[1]*Dictionary of Pentecostal and Charismatic Movements.* Synan, H. V., "William Joseph Seymour," pp. 779-781.
[2]Ibid., p. 780.

3

The Results of Faith

The total results of the Azusa Street revival will not be known in this life, as I wrote before. But look at the results we can see:

• Within two years, a small prayer meeting of black people had exploded into a worldwide revival. Part of the reason God could use Seymour and his small group in such a way was the presence of a great hunger in Christians of the Los Angeles area for more of God.

The Hispanic Roman Catholics had been praying for revival, and many of them participated in the mission when it began. They helped fix up the building, providing lumber and labor for the altar, benches, and repairs on the building, which was two thousand and four hundred square feet.

The impact, or the results, of this small prayer meeting were not evident in the beginning. I have already told you what the newspapers were saying, which many Christians joined in, I am sorry to say. Even a year later, well-known Christians would write that Azusa Street was receiving a lot of publicity but the meeting was having no effect on the city at large. The results of world-changing faith are not always immediately visible in the natural.

Apparently, however, those observers missed the fact that before a year was over, many mainline churches in Los Angeles were being stirred to revival. For the first time, many of them began to hold prayer meetings, to set "secret prayer" projects, and to work with city officials to hold street meetings. Finally, in March, 1907, there was a city-wide evangelistic meeting with guest ministers coming to speak from all over the United States.[1]

• From 1911-1914, three major denominations were started: the Assemblies of God, the United Pentecostal Church ("Jesus only"), and the Church of God in Christ. Other denominations founded in the next twenty years also had their roots in Azusa Street, such as Aimee Semple McPherson's International Church of the Foursquare Gospel (ICFG).

Many other denominations split into two groups: those who received the message of Pentecost and those who did not. Also, too many independent missions and churches to name were founded by people who experienced Azusa Street. Nearly every Pentecostal work today can trace its roots to Seymour's mission.

• The world once again had to choose whether or not it would receive the *whole* Gospel of Jesus or whether it would repudiate it as the scribes and Pharisees did. By 1914, the devil had to start a world war to try and stop the move of God.

• By 1990, it is estimated that more than three hundred and seventy-two million people were involved in the Pentecostal movement, which is directly rooted in Azusa Street. Church historian and statistician David Barrett says that more than four hundred million people were professing Pentecostals or Charismatics in 1990. The Charismatic movement of the 1960s was simply an extension of Pentecost from

Azusa Street to a new generation and to denominations that would not receive it in the early days of this century.[2]

These results can be traced back to the faith of Seymour and other ordinary people like him. He was full of faith, and God used him in a very powerful way.

• Another immediate result of the move of God at Azusa was that people came to church at *any time of day*. We think it is hard to go two or three times a week. Those services continued day and night and those eight hundred seats were like revolving doors. People who had been blessed were leaving and others were arriving.

• Another local result was the change in peoples' attitudes to giving. They never took up offerings during those services. There was a large, tin mailbox nailed to the back wall with a sign over it that said, "Settle With the Lord." Most church historians believe almost one hundred percent of the people who attended paid tithes — compared to about eighteen or twenty percent of Christians who pay tithes in the United States today.

When people truly believe that *without faith it is impossible to please God* (Heb. 11:6), you do not have to pull on them to give. People gave in that meeting because they had met the Lord there. When they saw the healings and other things that happened, they knew they were seeing a *miracle in motion*. The Godhead became very real to them.

Tithing does not make sense to the natural mind. When I was a child and had to pay my tithe, I felt badly every time.

I would think, "I just gave away money that could have helped buy my Little League cleats," or something to that effect.

That shows you that, when you are an adult with those thoughts, you are still a spiritual baby. You are thinking childishly, not childlike, as Jesus said. *Childlike* means perfect, innocent faith; belief without proof because you trust the one who tells you implicitly. Childlike means being humble. (Matt. 18:4.) *Childish* means "soulish," according to the flesh, selfish, not acting in a mature way and thinking first of self.

So, you see, one criteria for *great* faith is humility; another is trust in God.

Therefore a Christian who resists or resents paying tithes, which God said robs Him (Mal. 3:10), is showing distinct signs of being a "babe in Christ," as Paul wrote to the Corinthian church. (1 Cor. 3: 1-3.)

When you begin to mature spiritually and walk in faith, then you begin to see that tithing and giving make sense. However, first, you must want great faith desperately. You must set out on a quest for great faith.

The Quest for Faith

If you want your faith to grow, start at Romans 10:17, where Paul wrote that *faith comes by hearing.* Hearing what? Television? Radio? Movies? No, faith comes by hearing *the Word of God.* There are two words I want you to understand and remember concerning the quest for faith: *create* and *build.*

There is a difference between creating and building. A lot of times, we do things to *build* our faith. But building only seems to last a little while. Your faith can be increased, or built, through hearing a testimony of someone else's miracle in motion. You can build faith by reading good books about God and about His Word.

But only by reading the Bible itself can more faith be created. Through His Word and through prayer (communication with God), He creates faith within you. That is *more* faith, a greater level of faith, not simply "building," or expanding, what you already have.

John 15:7 says that if you abide in Jesus and His words abide in you, then you can ask what you want, and it will be given you. But that level of faith — which I call "divine" faith — only comes through His Word actually being so much a part of you that it is alive in you.

Faith hears the inaudible. In other words, when you move out in faith, you will more than likely have an *impression* from your spirit man of what to do. Few people, even great leaders, actually hear a voice. When most of them say, "God told me," or "God spoke to me," usually they mean what the old-fashioned church people used to call "a witness." They had an impression to do or say something.

You also might call it a "peace" or "a lack of peace." Suppose you go house hunting in "faith" that God will show you the right one. You walk into one that looks perfect, but inside is an uneasiness, a lack of peace. If you ignore that and buy it because your soul likes it, you probably will end up with a "lemon" in one way or another.

Your faith was made dead by not acting on it and substituting soulish desires (lust of the eyes) for your impression.

One day when I was just edging into the area of healing, I said to God, "Father, I am afraid to step out into the realm of healing, because I don't like to be rejected. Who wants to look like an idiot in front of thousands of people?''

People sometimes get in the healing line and look at me as if to say, ''I dare you to heal me,'' or, ''You aren't such a big deal!''

God showed me a little vision. I saw myself stepping out and God putting a rock under me. All I saw was water, but I took another step — and God put another rock under me.

Another time I said, ''God, why is it that, in some meetings, I am moving in so much more power and faith than in others?''

God said, ''It is because you have seen how many rocks I have put down, and then you begin to run by faith, knowing I am going to keep on putting down rocks.''

When faith begins to grow, your miracle is birthed in your spirit, but the flesh has to wait for the manifestation. That requires a great deal of patience and much standing in faith on the promises. When God speaks a word to you, or you claim a promise from the Word, you need to continue to stir up your faith or you will lose heart and faint before the manifestation of God's provision.

Another thing to remember in your quest for faith is not to mix spiritual direction with soulish thinking, or your progress toward the manifestation of the promise will be hindered.

Abram was called by God out of his country, and He believed God with ''a measure of faith'' to fulfill what He had promised. However, Abram also *acted*. He put legs to his faith by getting up and leaving Ur of the Chaldees. (Gen. 12:1.)

Now the Lord had said unto Abram, Get thee out of thy country, and from thy kindred, and from thy father's house, unto a land that I will shew thee.
Genesis 12:1

God had spoken to Abram; the Spirit led him in the right direction; but then, Abram's soul got involved. He took his nephew along. God told Abram to get up and go, to have faith in His word — but God never told him to take family along. In fact, God told Abram explicitly to leave his country, his people, and his father's household, of which Lot was a member.

In the realm of faith, the enemy throughout history has tried to get us to mix spiritual things with soulish things — if he cannot get us to totally deny or disobey God.

I am sure that Abraham listened to seemingly good thoughts about all this.

He probably thought, "Lot is my brother's child. This is the least I can do for him. I hate to leave him here in this godless place."

A lot of God's people have "Lots" or "barnacles" stuck to them that hinder their work for God. You can see from the events that happened to Abram that mixing his false compassion and sentimentality with a leading from the Spirit caused him to become double-minded.

Pretty soon, he moved into Pharaoh's area where, instead of a blessing, he became a curse because he lied about his wife. Instead of continuing in faith, Abram first got into fear. He thought Pharaoh might kill him to get his beautiful wife, Sarai.

A little later, he moved into Philistine territory and pulled the same thing on its ruler, Abimelech. This time, Abimelech almost got killed because of

Abraham's double-mindedness. I believe Abraham was supposed to go by himself and never was supposed to take Lot. I believe that because Lot never changed his ways. He never turned toward God to become full of faith like Abraham.

Lot's "spirit," or attitude, flowed over onto his own herdsmen, while Abram's attitude of heart was contagious where his herdsmen were concerned. But the confrontation of those two opposite kinds of hearts brought confusion. The herdsmen began to fight, so Abram allowed Lot to choose which part of the land he wanted.

Lot was a little entrepreneur, who tried to rip off his old uncle. And the Bible says that *the land could not sustain both Abram and Lot.* When God calls you to His purpose and plan and gives you a promise, He does not mean that for your entire neighborhood. He does not necessarily mean that promise for your whole family.

If God calls you to start a church or ministry, you need to let Him also choose your staff and your leaders. After all, it is *His* church or ministry. He is only calling you to be a steward over it. He does not mean your entire family is to be on staff. He does not mean every relative you have ever known is supposed to live in your house.

When God calls you somewhere by faith, He will make provision only for the people He has picked personally and called out with you. What happens a lot of times is that people receive a clear call in their spirits, then they get fearful and begin to want natural support. They want to hire people who will always tell them they are okay and doing the right thing. Their souls want "yes-men," not God-men, who will disagree if they do not have a clear witness from the Holy Spirit on something.

I see businesses, and even homes, sinking because they have people on payroll or living there who are not supposed to be there. Fishermen periodically scrape the barnacles off their boats, so they can move more smoothly through the water and at a better speed. (Barnacles are small seawater organisms that attach themselves to the bottom of a boat. Eventually, if there are enough, they cause a "drag" on the boat, and they contribute nothing to its welfare.)

You notice that nothing really happened in Abraham's life toward fulfilling that promise of a son of his own until after he separated himself from Lot, and after his faith grew from a measure, to a little and, ultimately, to great faith. Abraham, just like us, had to follow God's progression through the levels of faith.

Different Levels Bring Different Results

God honors faith at whatever level you operate. No faith brings no results; little faith brings little results; but, great faith changes your world. People unusually blessed by God have had unusual faith. That means they actually *believed* what God said did happen and would happen.

From Hebrews 11:6, we see two things:

1. We must believe (know) that God exists.

2. We must know that He rewards those who earnestly (hungrily, fervently) seek Him.

> **Without faith it is impossible to please him: for he that cometh to God must believe that he is, and that he is a rewarder of them that diligently seek him.**

In Romans 12:3, Paul wrote that God gives to every man *a measure of faith*. So when you say some

Christian has "no faith," that is not exactly true. That person was given the same measure as everyone else. What you mean is, "That person is not even using the measure of faith he was given."

Secondly, there is weak faith, or "little" faith. In Romans 4:19, Paul wrote that Abraham was "*not* weak in faith." Therefore he did not consider his own body, which was "dead," nor Sarah's womb, also "dead," but Abraham believed God.

Several times Jesus said to the disciples, "Oh, ye of *little* faith!" (Matt. 6:30,8:26,14:31,16:8, and in the other gospels.) He said that when He taught on believing God to feed and clothe them, when He had to wake up in the back of the ship to rebuke the winds and waves for them, when Peter began to sink even after walking a short way on water, and when they did not understand Him concerning the leaven of the Pharisees.

Also, there is *growing* faith. That means you are exercising your faith so that you are in God's progression, or pattern, of development. You are moving up from one level of faith to another. Look at what Paul wrote to the Thessalonians:

> **We are bound to thank God always for you, brethren, as it is meet, because your faith *groweth* exceedingly, and the charity** (love) **of every one of you all toward each other aboundeth.**
> **2 Thessalonians 1:3**

The Apostle Paul was excited because the church at Thessalonica was beginning to grow up. When your faith begins to grow, your love for God and your brothers and sisters in Christ also will begin to grow.

Paul also wrote about *great* or *strong* faith:

> He (Abraham) **staggered not at the promise of**
> **God through unbelief; but was** *strong in faith*, **giving**
> **glory to God.**
>
> **Romans 4:20**

Finally, there is *perfect* faith. Look at James 2:22,24, which again is referring to Abraham:

> **Seest thou how faith wrought with his works,**
> **and by works was faith made** *perfect*?
>
> **Ye see then how that by works a man is justified,**
> **and not by faith only.**

You see that *perfect* faith really means mature faith, perfected through step by step of hearing God, believing God, *acting* on that belief, and then moving on to believe for something greater. Then you are what Luke referred to when stating that Stephen was "full of faith." (Acts 6:5.) Stephen, the first Christian martyr, was full of faith and full of the Holy Spirit. I expect the two go hand in hand. Are you *full* of the Holy Spirit or just *baptized* in the Holy Spirit?

If you are *full* of the Holy Spirit, having given most areas of the flesh and soul over to the authority of the Lord, you will have few hindrances to walking in great faith.

Since some believers were not totally yielded to the authority of the Lord, division hit the church at Azusa Street and God's move was quenched. People began to walk in the soulish realm and fight about various things. They got into "power plays" about who was going to run the church. Division reveals rebellious spirits. There are people like Absalom, who want to kick their spiritual fathers off the throne and "rule" in their place. That allows witchcraft to enter. (1 Sam. 15:23.)

Because of things that happened after the first few years at Azusa Street, many people believe Seymour died of a broken heart at fifty-two years of age.[3]

The people who become involved in a move of God can stop it in spite of the leader with great faith. He, or she, can be used by God to start something moving. However, after enough people get involved, the momentum of that revival can be turned by the enemy to the right or the left, depending on how many people will listen to him instead of God. When that happens, the movement dies. It either becomes a "monument" to the past or it goes "flaky," and dwindles down to a few people. The end result in either case is death.

So do not ever believe that only the heroes and heroines count. *Every* person involved in a move of God is a hero or heroine used by the Holy Spirit, or they are weapons used by the enemy against the Lord's plan. *You* count, and even if you are never heard of by the world, you can make a difference by holding the line against gossip, division, or doubt.

The pastor of one of the country's largest churches told me once that the anointing on some of the preachers today is not any less than what was on those leaders of Azusa Street, the Healing revival, or other moves of God.

He said, "The difference is not the leaders but the people. The people of those moves had a great expectancy, a real desperation for God. Today, even the Church world is not desperate enough for the things of God." This kind of desperation will take you into a higher dimension of faith and cause you to believe for greater results.

Faith Rests on Knowing God

In order to be hungry for God, you must know God. It is not enough to be born again or even filled with the Spirit. Without Jesus in your heart and the Holy Spirit filling your life, you cannot be a child of God or have the power to grow into maturity. Without Jesus, you cannot know the Father; and without the Holy Spirit, you cannot move in the fullness of His power in the earth. Those things come first. However, neither of those relationships substitutes for a relationship with, and knowledge of, the Father.

After you become a child of God, you need to begin to find out Who He is, what His ways are, and what He likes and dislikes. If you truly love Him, and do not just lean on the fact that He loves you, you will develop a great hunger for a quality relationship with Him.

One reason a lot of Christians do not know God well is because they have tried to get to know him only through a man. In the beginning of your walk with the Lord, it is good to be able to see Jesus in men and women of God. Paul even wrote once to follow him as he followed Jesus. (1 Cor. 11:1.) However, no matter how spiritually mature and sanctified men and women of God are, no one is totally perfected yet.

Anyone can miss it, inadvertently hurt or wound you, or in some area give you a wrong impression of God. The Bible says you can come boldly to the throne of grace to obtain mercy. (Heb. 4:16.) Seeing Jesus in other Christians simply is God's way of giving you glimpses of Himself, in order to stir up the hunger in you to know Him better for yourself.

Most people have a second-hand revelation of God. They understand God through their pastors, their parents, televangelists, and so forth. So when things happen in their lives, they have weak, little, or no faith. You must *know* God personally to have faith in Him.

In our churches, we are teaching spiritual warfare before we teach people to understand God. I think we have the cart before the horse. I believe there should be a standard three-year course for most Christians in understanding and knowing God before they move into spiritual warfare, the gifts of the Spirit, or any extended ministry. Now, I do understand that some people can move into an intimate relationship with the Lord quicker than that, but in general, it takes that long.

The foundation stone on which faith rests is understanding and knowing God. You cannot erect a great tower on sand or without a solid foundation that will support it. You will begin to flow in God in an unusual way when you can think as God thinks, see as God sees, and "hear" direction and guidance in your spirit from Him through the Holy Spirit.

The Bible is the language of God. He literally talks to us through it. That is why I never pray without first reading the Bible. Then I pray back the scriptures and say, "This is what You said, Father. I'm just talking to You about what You said." Then I can begin to feel something happening.

The Word says that people who know their God shall be strong and carry out great exploits. (Dan. 11:32.) That means they press into God, go deeper into a knowledge of Him. Then, He says, they shall be strong because He gives them strength, and they will do great things. You take care of the depth of your relationship with God, and He takes care of the breadth of your ministry in His Kingdom.

Notes

[1]*Dictionary*, ''Azusa Street Revival,'' p. 35.
[2]Ibid., ''Global Statistics,'' pp. 812,813.
[3]*God's Glorious Outpouring* (Video).

4

Ten Facts About God

In order to know and understand God, you need to know some facts about His character and His personality. [Did you even know that God, Jesus, and the Holy Spirit have personalities? They must, because *we* have personalities, and we are made in God's image. (Gen. 1:26.)]

The Word says that, under the New Covenant, we need to "walk out" day by day being conformed to the image of Christ. (Rom. 8:29.) When you are born again, you receive the *nature* of Jesus within you. You become a new creature. (2 Cor. 5:17.) Your spirit man, the real you, has the life of God as part of you. That is the spiritual life and nature that Adam and Eve lost.

You already are generally conformed to God in the natural creation. For example, you have a brain, a soul (a mind, will, and emotions) and a spirit man. When you are born again, you receive Jesus and the nature of God as a free gift. So, what does it mean for *you* to "be conformed" to Christ? That sounds as if you have to *do* something, and we can do nothing about salvation but accept it.

What that verse means is that we must make choices day by day to think, act, and live as Jesus did and not according to the "old man" (Eph. 4:22; Col.

3:9), which we inherited from Adam and Eve. We must conform to the *personality* of Jesus.

There is nothing wrong with the soul as God created it; what is wrong are the things we have put into the soul. Things such as negative attitudes, focus on self, jealousy, competition, and so forth — all of the things Paul kept writing to the early churches to give up and stop doing.

What Paul was saying is that Christians should make choices that will transform their old personalities into a likeness to Christ.

Have you ever seen someone get saved in a total commitment and surrender to the Lord? Almost immediately everyone is talking about how they have ''changed,'' how they are not the same person. What has happened is that they have been conformed to the image of Jesus, and they have a *new personality*. However, most Christians have not surrendered all of their minds and emotions when they surrender their hearts. As a result, they must ''walk out'' the conforming process.

How can you make those choices if you do not know what Jesus was like on earth and is like today? You see, if you know Jesus, you will know the Father. That is what Jesus said. Therefore, in order to know God, you must study His Word. You must find out what He said about this thing and that, how He handled situations, and why sometimes there was mercy and sometimes judgment.

Abraham was called God's friend, because he ''cut a blood covenant'' with God and had a special fellowship with God. But Abraham got to know God *over the years* while he waited for the fulfillment of the promise. Moses wanted to know God's ways. He spent time with God and was privileged to "see God face to face" (a figure of speech for Moses' being allowed to see God's back passing by, as explained in Ex. 33:23).

David was another Bible person who began to develop a fellowship with God from his youth while tending sheep. Many of the psalms David wrote reveal God's character and ways. To develop an intimate fellowship with God, the psalms are a good place to start.

I am going to list ten facts you need to know about God and then talk about them briefly. All of these facts have more than one scripture that reveal them; however, I have selected only a few that are representative. They are:

1. God is a Person. He is real and has a personality. (Heb. 1:3.)

2. God is a Spirit, not made of natural matter. (Dan. 7:9.)

3. God can get angry. (1 Kings 11:9.)

4. God is a jealous God, and that is jealousy in the positive sense, not the negative. (Ex. 20:5.)

5. God hates certain things. (Ps. 101:3, 119:104,113,128,163; Prov. 6:16-19; Amos 5:21; Hos. 9:15; Zec. 8:17; Rom. 9:13.)

6. God loves. (John 3:16.)

7. God pities and grieves. (Ps. 103:13, 95:10.) The Bible even says that **Jesus wept** (John 11:35).

8. God is full of joy. (Neh. 8:10.) The fruit of the Spirit is part of God's personality, because as the Holy Spirit and Jesus are, so is God. (Gal. 5:22,23.)

9. God is intelligent. In fact, He is omniscient (all-knowing). (1 Sam. 2:3; Job 21:22.)

10. God is quiet and full of peace. (1 Kings 19:11,12; James 3:17.)

An evangelical organization in California is filling their churches and civic stadiums for combined meetings. They are having bigger meetings than any Charismatic group. Why? What is happening? One of my Pentecostal friends asked me how they were doing this without the gifts and power of the Holy Spirit.

I said, "Because they are being 'down to earth.' They are touching people where they live. They are showing people who God really is and that inner hungers can be satisfied by knowing God."

As Charismatics, we have focused on God's provision for our outer needs. Those things are important, and people needed to know that God's power and the gifts of the Spirit are for today. But we have almost lost our balance. Our feet must be on the Rock, Christ Jesus, not on what He can do *for* us.

Sometimes I think we show the world a God who does not seem to know what He is doing or what He is talking about! We need to be revealing a God who is real to the world. In studying the ten facts I mentioned before about God, let us pause and reflect a little longer on each fact in order to gain a better understanding of the reality of God and of *Who* He really is.

God is a Person:

> God, who at sundry times and in divers manners spake in time past unto the fathers by the prophets,
>
> Hath in these last days spoken unto us by his Son, whom he hath appointed heir of all things, by whom also he made the worlds;

**Who being the brightness of his glory, and the
express image of his (God's) *person*, and upholding
all things by the word of his power . . . .**
                                                    Hebrews 1:1-3

Will ye accept his *person*? . . . .
                                                    Job 13:8

The *express* image means the "exact" image of God
as a Person.

One of God's names is *I Am*. When Moses wanted
to know what name to give the Israelites, God said:
I Am That I Am (Ex. 3:14). So Moses said to Israel:
I Am **hath sent me unto you** (Ex. 3:14).

That means God is a Person who has existed from
the eternal past and who will exist forever in the eternal
future. The totality of everything in the universe is
wrapped up in Him to such an extent that He can sum
up His person, character, nature, ways, and whatever
remains in two simple words: *I AM*.

You also can know that God is a Person, because
the Bible talks about Him sitting (Dan. 7:9) and
speaking — all through the Bible He spoke to people
and He speaks to us today.

How could a non-person speak? He actually came
to earth and walked in the Garden east of Eden in the
cool of the day to have fellowship with Adam and Eve.
(Gen. 3:8.)

We need to stop thinking about God as a "force"
or an abstract being that is mostly "theological." If you
want to know Him, you must understand that He is
a real Person — the First of all persons.

God is a Spirit:

Jesus talked about the Father being a Spirit when
He visited with the woman at the well in Samaria:

**God is a Spirit: and they that worship him must
worship him in spirit and in truth.**
John 4:24

That simply means that God is made up of
supernatural matter, invisible to the natural eye. As
human beings, we are also spirits who live in natural
bodies, which are called the "temples" of God since
the New Covenant was ratified. (1 Cor. 3:16.) The devil
and his demons are spirits. The spirit body is the
eternal one, the lasting one, the one that is true reality.
The material realm is temporary and vanishes away.
Sooner or later, all of it dissolves back into the earth's
resources out of which everything was created.

**While we look not at the things which are seen,
but at the things which are not seen: for the things
which are seen are temporal; but the things which are
not seen are eternal.**
2 Corinthians 4:18

**For we know that if our earthly house of this
tabernacle were dissolved, we have a building of God,
an house not made with hands, eternal in the heavens.**
2 Corinthians 5:1

**Through faith we understand that the worlds
were framed by the word of God, so that things which
are seen were not made of things which do appear.**
Hebrews 11:3

God can be angry:

God is slow to anger, and He is so merciful! If we
had any idea how many of us as His children offend
His righteousness and His perfect will, we would never
cease marveling at God's forebearance, patience,
longsuffering, mercy, compassion, and grace.

However, there are certain things that transcend
even God's mercy and, at which, He becomes angry.

We need to clearly understand the things that are so anti-God that they can make Him angry:

• God is angered when His chosen leaders are not upholding Him and His Word before the people.

• God is angered when His enlightened leaders, who have tasted of an intimate fellowship with Him and who truly know He is the Great I AM, fall into idolatry.

• God is angered when His people offer up their children to the devil, use enchantments and divination (get involved in the occult), and **give themselves to do evil in the sight of the Lord** (2 Kings 17:17.)

An example of leaders not upholding God's Word is Moses and Aaron at Kadesh. God was angry at Moses for striking the rock instead of speaking to it when the Israelites wanted water. (Num. 20:11.) Once before, at Horeb, God had told Moses to *strike* a rock to bring forth water (Ex. 17:5,6); however, this time, He had said, "Just *speak* to it."

Moses said in Deuteronomy 1:37 that the Lord was angry with him because of the Israelites' rebellion and lack of faith in God. However, that is not what God said. God's character is not to be angry with one person because of what others do. What Moses meant was that the Israelites had provoked him so sorely that *he* lost his temper at them and exceeded God's directions.

Therefore we can see that God might be angry with you for blaming your shortcomings on other people and justifying your own behavior. God rebuked Moses *and* Aaron because *they* did not believe Him and *sanctify* (ratify, uphold His Word) Him before Israel. And, consequently, He said, neither Aaron nor Moses could go into the Promised Land. (Num. 20:12.) We often forget that Aaron was also included in this judgment.

You can "tempt" (provoke) God, because we were warned not to do that. (Ex. 17:2; Deut. 6:16; Isa. 7:12; Mal. 3:15; Matt. 4:7; Luke 4:12; Acts 15:10; and 1 Cor. 10:9.) God can be angry with leaders who do not "sanctify" Him before the people and do not believe Him, upholding His Word before them. I believe many people have not entered their "promised lands" because of such things.

However, I want to assure you of something: God is not mad at you. He is slow to anger. He will not always chide, nor will He keep His anger forever. (Ps. 103:9; Jonah 4:2.) That means He is quick to forgive when you repent. Israel tried His patience over and over, yet He always forgave them when they repented and turned from their wicked ways — until they went too far. He loved them all of that time; He simply hated what they were doing.

Finally, there came a time when God said to the Israelites, "Even if Noah, Job, and Daniel were living today, their righteousness could only save themselves. They could not intercede and hold judgment off the rest of you." (Ez. 14:14,20.)

Apparently, those three men were the most righteous of the Old Testament leaders. But do you see how long it took for God to become that angry? Hundreds of years. The same thing was true in Noah's day. God was not angry at David, who committed adultery, and at many other "heroes" — even Abraham — as I wrote earlier. He was grieved at their sins but not angered at *them*.

Many of His judgments did not occur out of anger but were handed down in sorrow. God said it was not His will or intention that any go to Hell. (Matt. 25:41; 2 Pet. 3:9.) He does not *send* people to Hell in anger — that was a wrong "theology" taught about God in earlier years and even in some places now. People send themselves to Hell by choosing not to receive the price Jesus paid for them.

All through the Bible, you will see people who made mistakes — God's people who sinned — and you will not read that God was angry with them.

If you take *one* of God's characteristics and emphasize that as if He is totally that and no other, you present a lop-sided, unbalanced picture of God. You do Him an injustice, and turn people away from Him rather than toward Him. What child, for example, wants to go to church where all he hears about is an angry, mean, vengeful God just waiting to smack him down?

No wonder we have lost a whole generation of young people, because they cannot relate to a God like that.

On the other hand, I would not want to keep on doing things at which God becomes angry. I would not want to trample on His grace, presume on His goodness and mercy, and continue in wicked ways.

The second thing in the Bible that shows God's anger is idolatry. First Kings 11:9 says specifically that God was angry with Solomon. Why? Solomon was no ordinary Israelite since he had experienced the advantage of David's knowledge about God. He had been blessed with natural prosperity beyond any other king Israel ever had. He had asked God for wisdom and was noted for wisdom all over the known world.

Rulers, such as the Queen of Sheba, came to Jerusalem just to sit at his feet.

Yet, he turned to idolatry, actually worshipping other gods for the sake of his foreign wives. As a result, we see that placing anything before God when you have had a taste of truly knowing Him can make God angry. Solomon repeated Adam's mistake. His weakness was his wives.

Also, God was angry with Aaron for giving in to the people and making the golden calf. Aaron's weakness was public opinion, or fear of man. (Deut. 9:20.)

When Israel — the ten-tribed northern nation — deteriorated to the extent of a widespread sacrificing of their children by placing them in the coals of fire to Moloch and participating so completely in satanic practices and worship, God was *very* angry and **removed them out of his sight: there was none left but the tribe of Judah** (2 Kings 17:18).

The fourth thing we see God angry at is the wicked. David said:

> **God judgeth the righteous, and God is angry with the wicked every day.**
> **Psalm 7:11**

These examples are enough to give you an idea of the kinds of things that make God angry. And you can see that He is not easily provoked, nor does He become angry quickly at His children. However, there are a number of scriptures that talk about God's anger being "provoked," or "kindled" by people's actions. Most usually, those things involved idolatry or stubborn rebellion.

God is a jealous God:

The first time in the Bible this characteristic is mentioned also shows us why God is so angry at idolatry. This verse concerns the First Commandment: **Thou shalt have no other gods before me** (Ex. 20:3).

> . . . For I the Lord thy God am a jealous God, visiting the iniquity of the fathers upon the children unto the third and fourth generation of them that hate me;
>
> And shewing mercy unto thousands of them that love me, and keep my commandments.
>
> **Exodus 20:5,6**

The Hebrew word translated *jealous* here is *qanna,* one of whose meanings is "very zealous."[1] The Apostle Paul used the same definition for *jealous* in 2 Corinthians 11:2, when he said:

> . . . I am jealous over you with *godly* jealousy.

There is a godly jealousy of protectiveness and caring, as well as an ungodly jealousy of possessiveness and control.

God hates certain things:

Proverbs 6:16-19 is a well-known passage that shows you the kinds of things God hates:

> These six things doth the Lord hate: yea, seven are an abomination unto him:
>
> A proud look, a lying tongue, and hands that shed innocent blood,
>
> An heart that deviseth wicked imaginations, feet that be swift in running to mischief,
>
> A false witness that speaketh lies, and he that soweth discord among brethren.

Proverbs is believed to have been written by Solomon. If he knew all of these things and had such knowledge of God, is it any wonder he provoked God to anger with his idolatry?

God loves:

Most Christians are familiar with the fact that John 3:16 tells us how much God loved the world (meaning mankind). However, His love is seen throughout the Bible. Another verse says that He loved us *while we were still sinners*. So obviously you can be a sinner and not be counted among the absolutely wicked whom God hates.

> **But God, who is rich in mercy, for his great love wherewith he loved us,**
>
> **Even when we were dead in sins, hath quickened us together with Christ, (by grace ye are saved).**
> **Ephesians 2:4,5**

God's anger is temporary, according to the Bible, yet His love is eternal. Jeremiah said:

> **The Lord hath appeared of old unto me, saying, Yea, I have loved thee with an everlasting love: therefore with lovingkindness have I drawn thee.**
> **Jeremiah 31:3**

Then John went beyond all of the scriptures about the love *of* God to say: **God *is* love** (1 John 4:16). That means that He does not simply have love, show love, and act in love, but that *love* is His innate nature, not simply an act, choice, or characteristic.

Again, as with all of these things about God, we should realize that, as we were made in His image, if we love, hate, are angry, feel pity, and so forth, we *had to get those things from Him*. Only the negative, wicked, ungodly things come from the influence of the adversary.

God has pity and grief:

David wrote that the Lord pities (feels sorry for, has compassion on) those who fear Him. (Ps. 103:13.) In fact, David wrote that God pities those people **as a father pitieth his children**. Other places in the Word of God, it says that God will *not* have pity on those who have provoked Him to anger and judgment.

James wrote that we can see God is very "pitiful" (full of pity) and "of tender mercy" in the conclusion of the story of Job where God restored much more than Job had lost to the devil. (James 5:11; Job 42:12,13.)

When the Word says that God "repented" that He had made man, that means God was grieved over man's wickedness to the point that He actually was sorry He had created us! Also, there was one man whom God so grieved over his attitude that He "repented" for having set him in office — that was King Saul. (Gen. 6:7; 1 Sam. 15:11)

God is full of joy:

Most of us are familiar with the verse from Nehemiah: **The joy of the Lord is your strength** (Neh. 8:10.) Psalm 16:11 says: **In thy presence is fulness of joy.** The Psalms are full of "rejoicing," which is expressing joy. Happiness usually comes from circumstances or surroundings, from the soul being content. However, joy flows out of the spirit man.

God is full of joy in spite of all of the horrible things happening on earth. We can allow joy to flow out of our spirits even in the midst of trouble and turmoil, because joy is not a temporary emotion. God always has been full of joy and always will be.

It may sound contradictory, but you can be sad about outward things, even troubled, and still be full of the joy of the Lord. That is what the disciples were doing when they rejoiced over being beaten for the Lord's sake. They were not rejoicing over being in pain and being humiliated. Outwardly, they were hurting, while inwardly there was great joy at having used the word of their testimony about Jesus consistently enough to bring on persecution.

God asked Job, "Where were you when I laid the foundations of the earth and the morning stars sang together and all the sons of God shouted for joy?" (Job. 38:4-7.)

Joy is a common state of being in the Kingdom of God.

God is intelligent and all-knowing:

There are many verses saying that God knows the hearts, the thoughts, and the works of man. Only God knows exactly how all nature operates and when the end of time is, according to Jesus. (Matt. 24:36.) God is the Creator who knows *all* things.

God is quiet and full of peace:

Elijah found out that God sends manifestations of His power in earthquakes, fire, and wind, but that God Himself manifests as **a still, small voice** (1 Kings 19:12). Job said that when God gives quietness, who can make trouble? (Job. 34:29.) How can He *give* quietness if He does not have it as part of Himself?

Isaiah wrote that the *work* of righteousness is peace, and the *effect* of righteousness is quietness and assurance. (Isa. 32:17.) God is all righteousness; therefore, His works are peace and the effect of His being is quietness and assurance to all who abide in Him.

Seek a Hunger for Him

I have tried very briefly in this chapter to stir up your desire to know more about God, to kindle a hunger for a *real* fellowship with Him, and to encourage you to study the Bible to find out about God. There are so many more aspects of His character and facets of His personality than I have shared here.

As you get to know more *about* God from His Word, your desire to know God personally should be sufficiently stirred to enrich your fellowship with God in your quiet times of devotion in His presence.

It seems to me as I travel all over the country that, in many churches, our services fall short of accomplishing what the Holy Spirit desires simply because we do not know the "moods," or the temperament of God well enough to discern what the Spirit wants to accomplish.

We still do things according to routine and tradition, even in Charismatic churches. We have simply discarded old denominational traditions to develop "new" ones. We may be doing warfare worship at a moment when God's plan is not to do warfare.

You do need to believe, however, that God's desire is to *have fellowship with you.* When you know that you are not in fellowship, be quick to do three things:

1) repent,

2) forgive yourself,

3) get up and continue in doing God's will.

Do not carry guilt and condemnation around with you. Those emotions are as damaging to a close fellowship with God as the sins and errors were in the beginning. They make barriers between you and God. If you truly believe He has forgiven you, why are you still dragging that shortcoming around? Let go of it!

Do not ever forget that, as a child of God, He is *on your side*, not against you. If God truly possesses you, and you possess Him, then He will bless you. Your faith can grow to great faith, and you can truly change your world, if you understand that aspect of your relationship with God.

Notes

[1]Strong, James. *The New Strong's Exhaustive Concordance of the Bible*, (Nashville: Thomas Nelson Publishers, 1984), "Hebrew and Chaldee Dictionary," p. 104, #7065.

5

God Blesses What He Possesses

God blesses those who have faith, and those who have great faith are His bondservants, as the Apostle Paul was. (Eph. 6:6; Tit. 1:1, NIV.) Overcomers are those who belong — body, soul, and spirit — to God, and Jesus made promises of special blessings to them in the book of Revelation. (Chapters 2,3.) Faith is hindered to the extent your flesh is involved in your daily walk.

There are at least twelve blessings, or personal results, of faith:

1. **Salvation.** (Acts 4:12.)

Salvation is the greatest blessing God has provided. But without a leap of faith, you cannot believe something that sounds so weird to the natural mind: A Being you cannot see is to enter your spirit, which you also cannot see, and cut off the dead skin around your heart (Rom. 4:11;) to make you a new creature. (2 Cor. 5:17.) That sounds like a fairy tale, a myth, or a legend to much of the world today. The only way to be justified and born again is by faith.

2. **Forgiveness.** (Luke 7:47.)

The woman, who probably was a prostitute (Jesus said her sins were ''many''), who anointed Jesus' feet with her tears, received forgiveness of sins because of her faith.

And he said unto her, Thy sins are forgiven.

And he said to the woman, Thy *faith* hath saved thee; go in peace.

Luke 7:48,50

It takes faith to *believe* your sins are forgiven. Somehow, our souls want to keep reminding us of past transgressions, and the devil helps that along. He magnifies condemnation, when Paul wrote there *is* no condemnation for those whose sins are forgiven. (Rom. 8:1.) Without great faith, you will not be able to let go of that remorse and feel truly washed clean.

Forgiveness — being as clean of something as if you had never done it — certainly is one of the greatest blessings of God. If you are still hanging onto past sins, God does not "possess" you, so you cannot receive the blessing of forgiveness.

3. **Righteousness.** (Rom. 4:22.)

Paul wrote that because Abraham *believed* (had great faith in) God, it was counted to him for righteousness. (Gal. 3:6.) God blesses those who have faith in Him with righteousness. When you believe Jesus enough to surrender your heart to Him and ask Him to come into your spirit, you receive His righteousness for your "filthy rags." (Isa. 64:6.) That is part of the Blood Covenant, the exchanging of cloaks by the two parties involved. Without great faith, no one could be born again and become "the righteousness of God." (2 Cor. 5:21.)

Look at how plainly Paul made this doctrine of God:

> **What shall we say then? That the Gentiles, which followed not after righteousness, have attained to righteousness, even the righteousness *which is of faith.***
>
> **But Israel, which followed after the law of righteousness, hath not attained to the law of righteousness.**
>
> **Wherefore? Because they *sought it not by faith*, but as it were by the works of the law. For they stumbled at that stumblingstone.**
>
> **Romans 9:30-32**

So, you see, works without faith are useless, and faith without works is non-effective (dead). There is no righteousness without faith. God blesses what He possesses, and if you are trying to *earn* righteousness, He does not possess you.

4. Justification. (Rom. 3:23-26, 4:5-8, 5:18,19.)

By *faith*, you receive Jesus and are justified as if you had never sinned. *Justification* may not be a term you have heard much in today's Church. However, it was very important to the Apostle Paul. That is the word he used in some form thirty-one times in his epistles.

It means God's grace in remitting (wiping out the penalty of) the sins of the ungodly and *imputing* righteousness to all those who receive Christ *by faith*. Actually, a short definition of *to justify* is "to declare righteous." It is a judge acquitting you of some crime of which you have been accused and, in addition, giving you legal immunity from ever being charged with that crime again!

5. Healing for the body. (Matt. 8:17.)

God has dominion over heaven and earth, and when He says something, it will come to pass. He gave all authority to Jesus, and Jesus delegated it to us. (Matt. 28:18; Mark 16:15-18.)

The word translated *power* in the *King James Version* is translated *authority* in the *New International Version*. It is *exousia*, which means "power, authority, control, dominion," and other like meanings.[1]

Through the stripes that Jesus endured before the crucifixion, He made a way for those who receive Him to be free from sickness and disease. (1 Pet. 2:24.) However, we must receive health and healing *by faith*. It is not automatically given to us any more than salvation is given to us without faith. James 5:15 says the *prayer of faith* shall "save" (heal) the sick.

6. **Miracles.** (Acts 6:8.)

Luke wrote about Stephen:

> And Stephen, *full of faith* and power, did great wonders and miracles among the people.
>
> **Acts 6:8**

Miracles are one of the gifts of the Holy Spirit (1 Cor. 12:10,28,29); however, from Luke's comment about Stephen and from Paul's epistle to the Galatians, it is obvious that *faith* also has a part. Yes, the Holy Spirit can move sovereignly, but most of the time, God intends for us to have a part in what He does — and that part is *faith*.

> He therefore that ministereth to you the Spirit, and worketh miracles among you, doeth he it by the works of the law, or by the hearing of faith?
>
> **Galatians 3:5**

7. **Daily food, having your needs met.** (Matt. 6:25-34; Phil. 4:19.)

In the Sermon on the Mount, Jesus talked about having faith in God to meet your daily needs. (Matt. 6:25-34.) He said that if God will clothe the weeds of the field, what makes you think He will not clothe you? Again there is that phrase: **O ye of little faith.**

Another place He said if your earthly father will give you good things and not give you a rock when you ask for bread, why can you not believe your heavenly Father will do even more? (Matt. 7:11.)

Paul wrote that God meets our needs according to His riches in glory, not according to our income or even the world's resources. (Phil. 4:19.)

However, once again it depends on how much time you spend in the Word of God, so that reading it, meditating, and hearing it can create faith in you toward God.

8. **Protection.** (Matt. 8:26.)

Jesus rebuked the disciples for little faith when He had to wake up and save them from the storm on the Sea of Galilee. The implication of His words is that, if they really had faith in Him, they would have been protected. We like to quote the ninety-first Psalm for protection from danger. However, even there, it takes faith, although faith is not mentioned. The very first verse says:

> **He that dwelleth in the secret place of the most High shall abide under the shadow of the Almighty.**

That means *faith*. If you abide in Him and know He abides in you, that knowledge is your faith working. You can be safe in His shadow.

9. **Stability, or being established in Christ.** (Col. 2:7)

Paul wrote to the Colossians about this blessing of God:

> **As ye have therefore received Christ Jesus the Lord, so walk ye in him:**

Rooted and built up in him, and stablished in the faith, as ye have been taught, abounding therein with thanksgiving.

Colossians 3:6,7

To establish means "to be stable, to be set firmly in place, to stand firm," and "to be strengthened."[2] Romans 4:20 says that Abraham was *strong* in faith ("strengthened in his faith," according to the NIV) and gave glory to God. Allow God to strengthen your faith and strengthen you *in* the faith (the Christian walk and beliefs). The two go together. The more you study the Word of God and the more you know Him through prayer, the firmer you are rooted on His doctrines. Then it will be easier for your faith to grow.

10. **Works of power through faith.** (1 Thess. 1:3.)

Without being given authority and power over the devil, we would not be able to do spiritual warfare. Therefore, God blesses those He possesses with delegated authority to overcome the devil, and He endues those who receive Him in the Person of the Holy Spirit with supernatural power to do great works and to overcome the enemy. (Luke 10:19, 24:49.)

Perhaps the greatest work of power is found in John 1:12,13:

But as many as received him, to them gave he power to become the sons of God, even to them that believe on his name:

Which were born, not of blood, nor of the will of the flesh, nor of the will of man, but of God.

"To as many as received Him" means all those who make that leap of faith to become born again. They possess Jesus, and He possesses them.

11. **Ability to do great exploits.** (Heb. 11:6.)

Elijah is an example of doing great exploits. How did he move from believing God for his daily needs to raising the widow's son from the dead? (1 Kings 17:17-24.) Remember? James said Elijah was an ordinary man like us. Concerning faith, he had to start where we start.

I like to think of faith as a rope or a chain, where each faith accomplishment adds another link. When Elijah was faced with the death of the boy, he simply pulled on the rope of faith that had been forged through his past blessings. He tied that rope firmly around him and had the strength to take on his next mountain.

You cannot "move a mountain" (Matt. 17:20, 21:21) if you have not been able to walk in enough faith to receive healing from a headache. Some people try to tackle a mountain on the basis of a word of prophecy or on the basis of what someone else did. It will not work. Your faith cannot be second-hand. It must be forged, link by link, into a strong chain connecting you back to God, from whom all of the promises come.

Also, you need to remember that it is not you who accomplish those things; it is the power of the Holy Spirit. Your faith simply makes a way for God to manifest His blessings and promises in your life. Faith is the "legal document" (title deed) that says you have a right to those things.

Faith is like a ladder, or a set of stairs, to use another metaphor. It is progressive. God does not take you through, or allow you to go through, all of the things you have experienced without a reason. If you trusted Him in each situation, He was creating a ladder of faith for you to keep climbing nearer and nearer to Him.

When I preach, I pull on the "rope" of past results of faith in my life. I begin thinking about all of the things God had done for me through faith in the past. I begin to see myself moving out across the "water" and God putting rocks under my feet.

I say to myself, "If God can help my mother raise five children with very little money, if God can deliver an alcoholic father, if God can teach me to read, if God can do what He did in other meetings, then He can manifest His power in such a way as to enable me to do great exploits for His glory and honor.

You may be in a spiritual dilemma — remember, God has delivered you out of previous ones.

You may be in a financial bind — think about all of the times God has made a way out for you. He did it before; He can do it again.

You must remember how far God has brought you. You may not be where you want to be, but, at least, you are not where you used to be. God has brought you a certain way, "line on line, precept on precept." (Isa. 28:10,13.)

12. **Victory over the world.** (1 John 5:4.)

We can overcome the things of the world through faith in the promises of God. We do not have to "sell out," compromise, or go the way of sinners in order to get along or get ahead in life. If we get to know the Lord well enough for our faith to be developed, we will believe that His blessings *can* come upon us and then we will experience victory in life.

But without faith, we cannot please Him. (Heb. 11:6.) You will get nothing from God without faith — not even salvation. You become a child of His through faith, and from then on, faith is the only "coin" or currency of the Kingdom of God. Faith is the only way you can get into a position for God to bless you.

I was reading in Psalms recently and ran across the verse where God said through David that we are not to take the way of mockers and scorners. (Ps. 1:1.) So many times young people enter the job market and think they have to lie a little or cheat a little in order to get ahead. Even in Christian colleges and universities, you can buy term papers. When I was in Bible school, there was cheating going on.

People lie about their taxes. They know all of the ways to get out of them. In reality, all of that is mocking and scorning the way of God.

Faith will enable you to do what is right and cope with the circumstances, whether they are difficult or easy.

Shipwrecked Faith: How *Not* To Get Results

Many Christians are not being blessed today, because they are not using their faith or are not developing it.

What happens is that most of us start off fresh with lots of faith. Then we lose the zeal, our first love. (Rev. 2:4.) We get in a spiritual rut and become shipwrecked or becalmed (sitting in a backwater not going anywhere), because faith must be continually stirred up.

If you want to maintain faith and even grow in it, you must keep it stirred up. I have noticed a lot of Christians who begin to think they have arrived, when they may have barely begun. They begin to think they are ''coaches,'' able to correct or direct any other Christians.

They tell the pastor how to act, the pastor's wife how to dress, the evangelist how to comb his hair, and so forth. After all, they have been "in the way" for thirty years. This is why you can get young Christians to do things that you cannot get older Christians to do many times — their faith is freshly stirred. Younger Christians have an easier time believing God will heal the sick or turn their worlds around.

Paul wrote Timothy that in the latter days, many would *abandon the faith*. (2 Tim. 3:1-7, 4:3-5.) We are living in the latter days. He told Timothy to "have nothing to do with them." That sounds uncharitable. Why would Paul say that? It is because those people who abandon the faith only had a "form" of godliness. (2 Tim. 3:5.) They have lost what faith they had.

After you have been in most churches for a while, you almost know what is going to be said or done. Someone can be talking, and your mind is a million miles away, but you can say "amen" at the right place. You can say, "Praise the Lord! Glory Hallelujah!" You know when to raise your hands during the praise and worship. You may be present in body, but you are absent in mind.

I remember the church we attended when I was young. Sometimes I would go to sleep, but I knew exactly when the pastor was going to finish his sermon. He always followed the same pattern: Begin fast, slow down in the middle, and get to preaching real hard at the end.

I would be half asleep and hear him pick up the pace. I would think to myself, "I'd better get awake and sit up straight. He's got about two more minutes."

That is having "a form of godliness." I was sitting in church and listening, but I was not *hearing* what the pastor was saying.

Paul became upset at people who had abandoned the faith. That happened a few times in Paul's writings. They departed from the faith, when they had been right with God in the beginning. There are some ministers today who have departed from the faith.

Any ministry that is more about building itself, or building up a person, than building the Kingdom, is departing from the faith. If you will notice, usually they have to resort to the world's methods of fund-raising also. God no longer "possesses" them, so they are not blessed. You cannot see the results of their faith. They are not changing the world but conforming to it in religious ways.

Following men and not God causes faith to deteriorate. Paul addressed that issue also. In 1 Corinthians 3:4, he wrote that some people in Corinth were saying, "I follow Paul," or "I follow Apollos," or "I am of the camp of Cephas (Peter)." All of them should have been following Jesus, not the gifts He had set in the Body to perfect them for the work of the ministry. (Eph. 4:11,12.)

Another thing that can happen to your faith is to allow it to be shipwrecked. (1 Tim. 1:19.) Look at all the other ways your faith can be nullified:

- Some will turn away. (Acts 13:8.)
- Faith can be made void (of no value). (Rom. 4:14.)
- Faith can be "cast off." (1 Tim. 5:12.)
- Faith can be abandoned. (2 Tim. 3:8.)
- Faith can be dead. (James 2:17.)

- Faith can fail. (Luke 22:32.)
- Faith can be made of no effect (have no results). (Rom. 3:3.)

One reason I believe God is calling men and women of God to challenge people concerning their faith is that many Christians are not progressing through the various levels of faith; they are allowing their faith to die. They have "dead," or dormant, faith.

Have you ever heard the expression used about someone, "The lights are on, but no one is home?"

Is Anyone Home?

That means the person is alive, breathing and moving, but you cannot get any sense out of them. They do not seem to be able to hear reason or operate in reason. The same thing can happen to a Christian. He can be born again, even Spirit-filled, going to Heaven: the lights are on, but no one is home. Those Christians have gone from a measure of faith to weak faith, little faith, and then dead faith. Those people are on the verge of being "cast away."

Sometimes I have prayed for a person, and it felt as if I had put my hand on a cold refrigerator. I have talked to other evangelists about this, and they have had the same experience. In those cases, we have come into contact with *dead faith*.

Dead faith says, "I'm not here."

No "juice" is flowing; no power is evident. Those people are one step away from backsliding. So many Christians today have not stirred up their faith; they have not let the Lord touch them; they have not tried to learn of Him, from Him, and about Him. They have little or no spiritual understanding. They do not know God as perhaps they used to know Him.

That is why a minister can be preaching the best stuff in the world with people looking at him and listening, but the message is flowing right over their heads and onto the floor. The lights are on, but nobody is home. Some preachers try to do a "song and dance" show to keep the people's attention. If the church was really on fire for God, you would not have to do all that. You could simply preach the Word.

People would be sitting on the edge of their seats saying, "Feed me! Feed me! I'm so hungry to know more about God."

When I first met my wife, I wanted to know all about her. I talked to this person who had known her since she was a child.

I said, "What is Cindy like? What kind of person is she? What kinds of guys does she date?"

I wanted to know everything I could about her. When you have active faith stirring inside you, when you really care about God, you want to know all about Him.

It seems as if the "deader" the faith, the more people sit back in their chairs and yawn. You pray for them or lay hands on them, and there is nothing there. It reminds me of a woman I prayed for in Chicago the first time I was there. It was a powerful meeting and powerful things happened.

God was moving mightily. Among those healed was this woman who was hurting and could not move, much less walk. The power of God hit her, and she started walking. The place went wild.

Then I said, "How do *you* feel?" (I was on Cloud Nine!)

And she said, "I feel good — but I don't know how I'm going to feel tomorrow."

Can you imagine that? If people are healed on my faith, and then the devil comes to try to put pain on them or put the symptoms back, and they have no faith of their own, they will lose their healings. The devil attacks you based on your faith. If you do not have the faith to challenge the attack, you may end up worse off than before.

Do not forget that the devil will always come and try to take back the territory you gained through fighting in faith. If you had a problem with cigarettes, sex, food, or addictive substances, the devil will try to get you to take that back at some time or another.

Why does he come back and try to get you on the same ground you beat him on? He does that because he is a "sore loser," as a great man of God told me once. Satan does not want you to have a victorious testimony.

Sometimes you feel like saying, "Hey, devil, I've got twenty-two other areas. Try working on them!" You can get so tired of fighting the same battles over again.

To have faith that can move mountains, learn to know God, believe His promises and blessings, and then "put feet to your faith."

Notes

[1]Goodrick, Edward W. & Kohlenberger, John R. III. *The NIV Exhaustive Concordance*, (Grand Rapids: Zondervan Publishing House, 1990), "Greek to English Index-Lexicon," p. 1719, #2026.
[2]Ibid, p. 1088.

6
Putting Feet to Your Faith

When we think about those who did great exploits for God, we think first of all of Enoch and Noah:

Enoch pleased God because of his faith, the Bible says. (Gen. 5:24; Heb.11:5.) He was translated because His faith *pleased* God. Being righteous in his day was a great exploit because of the society in which he lived. And pleasing God with your faith always is a great exploit.

Noah's building the ark in total faith and his obedience was a great exploit. You cannot walk in obedience to God unless you have great faith.

Noah was warned of God: *He heard God.* So he had to know God well enough to hear Him.

Then he received what he heard in godly reverence (fear, or awe, of God): *He believed what he heard.*

Thirdly, he obeyed: *He built the ark.*

By building the ark, he did what I call "putting feet to your faith." In other words, he translated faith into works. He combined believing with doing.

We cannot even imagine how much faith it took for Noah to believe an unseen Being, who told him the earth was going to be totally flooded with water. God said it was going to "rain." (Gen. 6:17, 7:12.) It

had never rained on earth before. There was a mist
that came up at night and watered the earth.

> . . . **For the Lord God had not caused it to rain
> upon the earth . . . .**
>
> **But there went up a mist from the earth, and
> watered the whole face of the ground.**
>
> **Genesis 2:5,6**

You can see the difficulty of belief by the fact that
no one else outside his family was able to believe it.

To believe the impossible, which is what that took,
you have to have a center of righteousness somewhere.
The rest of the world was so wicked by that time,
people were not able to make the stretch of imagination
to believe it. Noah, the Bible says, was righteous ("a
just man"), **perfect in his generations** (Gen. 6:9.) That
means he was in right-standing with God. He lived
right in a wicked world.

Godly reverence allows great faith to develop.
Godly reverence means having the proper respect for
God, and the right perspective: He is God, and we are
His creations. If you are a Christian, Jesus "owns" you,
because you were "bought with a price." (1 Cor. 7:23.)

Those who are humble enough to make a total
surrender — to be "bondslaves" — are the ones with
great and divine faith. They are the ones who put feet
to their faith to turn their worlds upside down for God
and whose exploits are known throughout the
Kingdom.

If you are a parent, does it concern you when you
tell your children something to do, and they do not
obey?

Does it concern you when they act as if you have
no idea what you are talking about and what you say
really does not mean much?

Then imagine how God feels about most of His children.

We need to revere God. We need to understand there is a proper respect, even for a loving Father — or perhaps *especially* for a loving Father. Much of the Church, in general, has gone from the extreme of believing God is a "meanie" to believing He is a "wimp." Both extremes are untrue.

When God says, "Pick up and move," for example, He means *now*, not later, or maybe. We need to do that out of respect if nothing else.

One commentary I read said it took godly fear for Noah to move on God's command. There is no way anyone is going to begin to build a big boat when no one has ever seen a boat that size, and no one has ever seen water pour out of the sky.

They probably said, "That flies in the face of every scientific principle we know! Whoever heard of water falling out of the sky? Noah, you have lost your mind. That is not possible. Do you think there are streams and rivers in the sky for water to pour out of?"

Noah did not understand what God was saying would happen any better than the others. But he had a godly reverence for God, so Noah believed the impossible and obeyed.

There was an occasion in one of my meetings when something happened in a service that would not have happened if I had not been obedient. I did not obey because I had "great faith;" I obeyed because of Godly reverence. I had none for that particular healing at that particular time. I thought it was not even possible in the climate of that service. But God was able to move, because I obeyed.

If "you know that you know that you know" you
are hearing God, obedience can substitute for faith. It
is putting feet to your faith, even when your faith is
not working. God honors it, because you are
accomplishing His purpose.

Obedience Puts Feet to Faith

I was holding a service in one of those churches
where it felt as if everyone's faith was dead, one of
those places that pulls the anointing right off you. It
was like Jesus' hometown, where He could do no
mighty works because of their unbelief. (Matt. 13:58.)

Usually, if you have a healing ministry, you learn
to look out over the congregation and discern whose
faith is at the level where healing can come. Otherwise,
if you pray for a half-dozen people and nothing
happens, everyone else's faith goes downhill. When
you are dealing with a crowd, you need to be very
careful that you pray first for those whose faith has
been created and can be contagious. Those results can
"build" others' faith to the point where they also can
receive.

In this service, I was in a "dead" church in the
middle of the message and had no healing anointing
on me. All of a sudden, this boy got up from the back
and began to walk up the aisle toward me very slowly,
using a walker. He obviously was very badly crippled.

I looked at him and wondered where the ushers
were! They were supposed to catch things like this.

Then I thought, "Oh, great! This is like running
from a standing start. At least, give me a cold or a
headache, not this kind of case. Don't give me
someone who is paralyzed!"

About that time, I felt the Lord say, "This is of Me," but I thought that could not be God. Surely that was the devil trying to break up the service, and I wanted to rebuke him. This was out of order in the natural, and I thought it could not be God — and, yet, somehow I knew that it was.

I said to God, "Lord, because I think this is of You, I am going to do what You tell me. But you know I have no faith. In fact, I do not believe anything is going to happen. These people are so dead in this service. I have no faith. They have no faith. But because I believe it is You, I am going to move out in obedience."

When the boy reached the front, I said, "What is going on? Why did you come up here?"

And he answered, "I was sitting back there, and I felt the power of God, and as you were giving the testimonies of healing, I just believed God could heal me."

You see, there *was* someone in the meeting with great faith, after all. And God met the boy's faith.

All the people were looking at me with the expression, "I dare you to try this one. Put your actions where your mouth is, great healing evangelist."

I asked the boy what had happened to him, all the while trying to keep my best I-really-have-faith face on. He told me he had been in an accident in which most of his bones were crushed. He had pins everywhere in his bones. His back was all messed up, and he could barely make it in a walker.

There was not even any anointing oil available. It was that kind of church.

In obedience, I said, "God, in reverence to You, I lay hands on this boy for healing" — and the power of God began to shake him.

I said, "What's happening?"

He answered, "Something's going through me," and I thought, "Boy, this is a shock to me!"

I did not feel anything, and if you have ever been in one of my services, you will know that I am usually the first to get excited at what God is doing. This time I felt nothing at all.

Suddenly, he dropped the walker and began to run. The place went wild, and it was almost as if God were saying, "I told you so." I was still standing there with no anointing to heal, watching all of this, and not feeling a thing.

So if you know God is telling you something you cannot believe with your natural mind, and you have no faith for it to happen, move out in obedience and trust God, because you are putting feet to your faith.

Another way of presenting this principle is this: *You cannot walk on water until you get out of the boat.*

Peter may have lost his faith, but it was a great exploit to even start out walking on water. None of the rest of the disciples did.

Take One Step at a Time

Another principle concerning translating your faith into action is to move out step by step, as we have seen God operate in the things He does. First, He created light, then the next thing and the next. (Gen. 1.) He did not create the whole world instanteously all in a snap of a finger. I am not saying He could not have done it that way if He had wanted. But He is a

God of order and organization. I believe He showed us in the very first chapter of the Bible that His way of doing things is "line upon line, precept upon precept." (Isa. 28:10,13.)

Noah began his faith walk by gathering the materials, then laying a foundation, and so on until he had the finished product. Take one thing at a time. Begin with small things and small areas. If you are believing God for a new car or a new house, take care of the ones you have. Make up your mind that your old car or your small house is going to be the cleanest and neatest one in the neighborhood.

Nothing happens overnight, but if you do not start now, nothing will ever happen. *Today's decisions are tomorrow's realities.*

When I was first called to preach, I had cards printed up that said, "Worldwide Evangelist," and I put those in my room so I could see them all of the time. I had never preached one time when I did that. No one would let me. But I preached in my room and saw thousands in front of me. By faith, the door knobs were getting saved! By faith, the couch was rededicating its life.

One day, my roommate walked in while I was preaching, and he said, "What are you doing?"

I said, "I'm preaching."

He said, "That's great. I feel the anointing in here."

I said, "Be quiet," and I kept preaching.

I thought, "For the last two weeks I have been preaching to nobody. Now at least I've got one person listening."

Then he said, "Tim, I want to preach. This is powerful. How long have you been doing this?"

I said, "For a while," and he exclaimed, "I want to preach here!"

So I said, "Okay, you go ahead and take this 'church.' It was getting too small for me anyhow."

You have to get out of the boat and walk by faith.

Remember in an earlier chapter we talked about the steps of faith we can see in Elijah's life? Sit, stand, walk, run, soar. You cannot soar in faith until you walk. You cannot walk until you stand, or stand until you sit. Most people never run in faith at all. Running is *moving out in faith passionately*.

The lady with the issue of blood sat and heard the Word of God. She stood and walked, then she ran. That is when she got hold of the hem of His garment, against her culture and her religion. Women did not touch men who were not their fathers, husbands, or sons. Also, according to the Mosaic law, the issue of blood made her unclean. She should not have been out in public at all, according to the Pharisees.

What she had was almost as bad as leprosy. Her husband could even have divorced her for it. But she heard that Jesus was in town, and she stood up in faith and walked out the principles.

"I'm going to the street meeting," she decided to herself.

She began to run in her faith when she came to the place where she knew that if she could just get to Him, she could be healed.

But she began to soar when she said to herself, "I don't care what it takes or what I have to overcome. I am *going* to get to Him."

When she touched the tassels on His cloak, she received the results of her faith. Her world was changed.

Soaring is having "the God-kind of faith":

> **And Jesus answering saith unto them, have faith in God.** ("Have the God-kind of faith.")

> **For verily I say unto you, That whosoever shall say unto this mountain, Be thou removed, and be thou cast into the sea; and shall not doubt in his heart, but shall believe that those things which he saith shall come to pass; he shall have whatsoever he saith.**

> **Therefore I say unto you, What things soever ye desire, when ye pray, believe that ye receive them, and ye shall have them.**
>
> **Mark 11:22-24**

The "God-kind" of faith is "divine faith" and "mountain-moving faith." That means you are so overwhelmed with God that you can believe the impossible. But you cannot begin at this stage. You must first learn to sit, stand, and walk.

Peter's faith when he healed the man at the Beautiful Gate was a progression. (Acts 3:1-10.) As the apostle who denied Jesus, Peter was still learning to sit. Yet a couple of months later, he was soaring in the God-kind of faith.

All through the gospels, you see Peter falling, getting up and starting again, and falling again. He was sitting, standing, walking out the principles of faith. He denied Jesus, and had to get up and start over. On the Day of Pentecost, you see him beginning to run, preaching in the greatest conference of all time. He saw thousands of people saved, and his confidence was built up. More faith was created in him, because he knew God was putting rocks under his feet. He did not have to worry about sinking in the water of life again.

After that, you see him as he began to pray for the sick. A few days after Pentecost, Peter and John were on their way to the temple to pray when they passed a man born lame. (v. 2.) And God gave Peter a "God-idea." Actually, it was a "word of wisdom" from the Holy Spirit. (1 Cor. 12:8.)

Jesus had walked that way many times, and He must have passed the same beggar. Yet He had no witness from God to stop and heal the man. Healing with most people is a matter of timing.

When Peter received that instant prompting from God that the man could be healed, he did not say, "I'm just a little fisherman from Galilee. I denied my Master three times. I can't do great exploits. I'm not worthy."

But neither did he say, "I am the only man besides the Son of God who ever walked even a few steps on water. I am the great preacher who preached on the Day of Pentecost and caused five thousand people to become new creatures in God."

He was humble and obedient, knowing that only through Jesus' name could anything be done for the man. So Peter pulled on that "rope of faith." He pulled the rope of blessings, reached out, and raised the man up by the right hand. Immediately, the Word says, the man's feet and ankle bones received strength. (v. 7.)

Obviously, the man had no faith. He did not even know what was going on. He was looking for money, not healing. If he had faith, probably he would have reached out to Jesus Himself as the lepers did (Luke 17:12) and blind Bartimaeus. (Mark 10:46.)

In the Greek, when Peter said, **Silver and gold have I none; but such as I *have* give I thee,** *have* means "such as I now possess" in the sense of someone possessing a new arm.

Peter was saying, "This faith in Jesus and power of the Holy Spirit I now possess is part of me, just as your new legs and ankles are going to be part of you. What I have is not something that comes and goes, but something that is as much a part of me now as if it had been born into my body.

"Now I *know* God can use the ordinary to do the extraordinary. I have now come to a top level of faith progression. I have that overwhelming faith bubbling up in me. I have pulled on my rope of blessings. God possesses me.

"Look at my eyes, lame man. I have Jesus Christ in me, the hope of glory, the Greater One, the resurrected King. He is the Healer, the Alpha and Omega (beginning and end). (Rev. 1:8.) He is the God who quickens the dead and calls those things that are not as if they already are. (Rom. 4:17.)

"I have the God who quickens the dead within me. I saw Jesus heal people and raise people from the dead. I saw Him cast out demons. I even saw Him raised from the dead! Do you think your physical condition can scare me?"

Of course, there are times in your walk of faith when you will fall down. But get up, learn why you fell, and make sure you never stumble over that thing again.

Walking in the spiritual life is no different than babies learning to walk in the natural. They fall, get up and try again, fall again, and so on until they can walk with strength. Sure, sometimes they get hurt — but they get up and try again.

If you can identify with what I am saying, I would like to say to you, "Welcome to the process of learning to soar."

Others Depend on You Soaring

Who got the most benefit out of Peter's soaring faith? It was not Peter, although he received blessings and his own faith was strengthened through this incident. It was one more section in his rope of faith. However, the lame man is the one who benefited most. The God-kind of faith is most of all for other people's benefit.

If you notice in the scriptures, all of the great exploits were for God's purpose or to help other people. They were not for the person with the faith. Even in Noah's case, the main reason for his being obedient was to perpetuate the human race. He was "righteous" in his generations. He could have gone on to be with the Lord without all of the difficulty of starting an entire world over.

You do need faith that God will meet your needs, protect you, and guide you. But that is not "mountain-moving" faith. That should not require more than a measure of faith, because we are told those things are ours over and over in the Word of God.

Everytime I begin to run or soar in faith, it is for someone else's benefit — or to fulfill something God has set me to do for Him. Believing for finances to maintain the church and ministry with all of the outreaches is for the Kingdom of God, not for me.

For example, at a recent meeting in Texas, I walked up to a girl with multiple sclerosis.

I said to her, "What would happen if I picked you up?"

She said, "I would fall straight to the floor."

I said, "How bad is it (the MS)?" and she answered, "Real bad."

Then I said, "Between me and you, I believe you are going to get up and walk tonight."

Now I did not say that into the microphone, but just to her privately. After that, I walked off and began to lay hands on people for back problems and arthritis, and my faith kept rising and rising.

After a while, God said, "Now, go get her."

And I said, "Give me that microphone!"

I took off my jacket and got the anointing oil. Then I grabbed her by the head and said, "You don't have a choice. Get up!"

I stood her up, and she started walking and screaming, "I can walk! I can walk!"

That is the God-kind of exploit, but it was for her benefit, not mine.

You can move that way in circumstances in your life. Start saying to the mountain that it has to move. Begin to tell your finances that you did not come this far to fail. You are not going bankrupt. You are not going to lose your house or your family. For the glory of God, you are going to keep making that rope of blessings. You are going to keep hanging onto it until you reach the God-kind of faith.

That is the boldness that few people ever learn to walk in. The well-known British evangelist Smith Wigglesworth walked in that place. A number of people were raised from the dead in his ministry. After his wife died, he lived totally and completely for God. He was totally "sold-out" to the Master.

Make a note of this:

Somewhere someone is waiting for you to soar.

Three sets of people waited for Elijah to soar during the famine: the widow who helped him and was able to live, her son, and their close family. The Bible says that not only was the son touched, but the family was touched. (1 Kings 17:15.)

If you do not walk in your miracle and put it in motion, nothing will ever happen. Perhaps many people need you to learn to soar in faith. If you do not get up from that dry brook and move out in the things God has for you to do, other people will suffer.

Developing your faith is not a one-time thing, nor is it something personal just for you. Faith is a chain-reaction, because God always works through people to touch other people. Think of all the people you can help with the finances He would give you through faith. If God can get you to develop the faith to do the missions project you are supposed to, think of all the people overseas who will be touched.

Someone is waiting for you to awaken that faith in yourself. They are waiting for you to soar. There is a great amount of responsibility that goes with the God-kind of faith.

Faith is not an option for us; it is a requirement for walking in the style of Jesus.

Noah's God-kind of faith was extremely important even to you and me. Because of Noah, all of mankind was saved. You and I were born because of Noah's faith.

Rahab is a classic case of this. Because she walked in faith, her whole family was saved. (Josh. 6:17,22-25.)

Because she walked in faith, she is one of the heroines of Hebrews 11. (v. 31.)

Joseph walked in faith, and his immediate family was saved in time of famine. The Egyptians were saved from famine. And God's Israelites got off to a good start toward being a nation.

Do not be discouraged because you do not have much faith now. Begin where you are.

Do not give up because no one will let you preach. Go out on the street corners.

Do not give up, even if you are in prison reading this. Sometimes those tough experiences are what build faith and give you determination. In order to move into the God-kind of faith, you have to first learn to "think big in small places."

7

Thinking Big in Small Places

You can look again at most of the Bible heroes and see that they thought big in small places. Elijah did one of his greatest exploits, the one we have looked at from several different aspects in this book, in the small home of a widow woman.

He was in a "small place" figuratively speaking when he — one man for the true God — faced hundreds of priests who were for Baal on the mountain top at Carmel. (1 Kings 18:17-46.)

Samson, the twelfth and last of Israel's judges, did the greatest exploit of his entire life in one building. He thought big while he was blinded, imprisoned, and used as a donkey to turn a grinding wheel. (Judg. 16:21.) He destroyed more of the enemy in his death than in his entire life. (Judg. 16:30.)

Paul and Silas thought big when they were beaten and thrown in jail, sitting in stocks. (Acts 16:25.) Earlier, the apostles had rejoiced that they were counted worthy to be persecuted and suffer shame for Jesus' sake. (Acts 5:41.) That *really* is thinking big in small places.

How many of us would think like that? Most Christians in America today would not rejoice over being persecuted. Rather, they would think it was not fair, complain, and resent it. Instead of thinking big in a small place, we would be thinking small and wasting an opportunity to grow in faith.

Dr. Paul Yonggi Cho, pastor of the largest church in the world (with more than three-quarters of a million people), thought big in a small place. That is how he built his rope of faith into the great exploits that he is doing for God.

When he began preaching as a young man, he was very poor, and he began to believe for a table and chair. He also was preaching to poor people. Later, he believed for a bicycle so he could visit his people.

He got up in church and said, "I'm so happy because God has given me a table and a chair," and his congregation began to cheer.

After the service, some young boys came up and wanted to see the table and chair, and Cho said, "Oh, I don't actually have them yet, but God has given them to me. Have you ever seen a woman who is pregnant?"

The boys answered yes, and Cho said, "Well, can you actually see the baby yet? Can you hold it? Of course not. But she *has* the baby already. It just is not yet visible. That is the way it is with my table and chair. I am pregnant with them."

Cho was going through the eye of faith that sees the invisible, calling things that are not as though they are. He was learning to sit.

Finally, he got his table and chair, and later, a bicycle the same way. Then he began to believe for a church, and as the years have passed, he has achieved the largest church in the world through a step-by-step progression of growing in faith.

Some of you reading this book have been given a vision of what you can do for God with finances, of what you are going to do on your job, of what you can do in the ministry. But that does not mean you will do those things overnight. You have to believe God is growing that thing inside of you. You have to start small, but think big.

My wife and I have been married several years, and we have lived in small places. But we have believed for a big house. We have been pregnant with it. Not only have we seen our house as already achieved, but we put feet to our faith by "seeding" into other people's homes.

We could have had several houses by now if we had not "invested" in other people and other ministries, but we knew these principles of faith. So we chose to wait on God's timing and be sure we got exactly the right house at the right time.

Finally, the Lord showed us the right house. We are restoring it exactly the way we want it. But while we were getting to this place, we lived in a small townhouse. All of the time, however, we thought big. As we traveled across the United States, we kept our eyes open. We looked at houses to see things we liked and did not like. We bought decorating books, books about houses, and other related subjects.

Over the years, people have said to me, "Tim, you are crazy for giving all that money away. You could live in a nice house."

I said, "Things may not happen when you want them to, but if you walk in faith, they always are right in God's timing."

Faith sees the invisible.

Faith hears the inaudible.

People say, "How do you know God is telling you to do something?"

It is not anything you hear, usually. It is something you "sense," an "impression," as I wrote in an earlier chapter.

While you are in small places, do not only think big but help others, encourage others. That means you are investing in other people's lives. I believe God is bringing back the gift of "exhorting" to the Church, the art of encouragement.

The Art of Encouragement

Many of the great heroes and heroines of faith walked without very much encouragement. However, encouraging was what Deborah did to Barak. Samuel tried to encourage Saul, but Saul would not receive it.

Paul knew how important encouraging one another is. That is what he and Silas were doing when they sang and rejoiced in prison. They not only were thinking big in that small place, but they encouraged one another. (Acts 16:25)

There are several places in Paul's letters where he stresses that Christians must exhort and encourage one another to continue in the faith. (Acts 14:22.)

Here are a few of those verses:

> But *exhort* one another daily, while it is called Today; lest any of you be hardened through the deceitfulness of sin.
>
> **Hebrews 3:13**

> And let us consider one another to provoke unto love and to good works:

> Not forsaking the assembling of ourselves
> together, as the manner of some is; but *exhorting* one
> another: and so much the more, as ye see the day
> approaching.
>
> **Hebrews 10:24,25**

I believe we are going to see more people like myself who know how important it is to exhort and encourage others. It is very hard to move through the progressive steps of growing in faith and to think big in the small places of life without someone to encourage you.

Personally, I know how important it is, because I received little encouragement during the days when I was in such a small place trying to preach.

Most people are so caught up in their own agendas, so worried about their own territories and their own lives that they do not have the courage — or feel good enough about themselves — to encourage someone else toward greatness. You can never encourage someone else unless you have a confidence in God about yourself.

When I was trying to move out of that small place of ministry and develop myself into what God wanted, I looked for men of God to help me. A few did, but many were not secure enough in themselves to reach out and encourage me.

I would walk up to them and say, "I want to be a man of God. I want to do this and that," and they would say, "That's great; that's super," and walk off.

My biggest encouragement came from women. I was raised by a mother and three sisters, and I have always respected women. So God raised up a woman to encourage me. A European woman saw potential in me, and even while I was a Bible student, she invited me to come to Europe and preach in some churches.

At that time, I had only preached six or eight times, and my largest congregation had been ten people. Yet she was inviting me to preach to crowds of from a thousand to twenty-five hundred people!

While I preached, she sat and prayed in tongues, because God had told her that she had history in her hands.

All the male preachers had seen me as just another young man excited about God, but God had told her something about me that was different. She also taught me many useful things, such as not allowing myself to be caught talking to girls or women alone. She showed me there was danger in the appearance of that, if nothing worse happened.

She taught me that if you are a leader, you do not have time to be everybody's buddy. You have to pray hard, study hard, and work hard. That is how you build your rope of faith.

Once she asked me to pray and intercede with all of these European people in the basement of a building.

I said, "I don't feel like it."

At that time, I was about twenty years of age, and I was with a pretty girl and some friends, having a good time. We were walking around talking while a group of people were interceding in the basement for this conference of from eight to ten thousand people.

That is where I should have been. I could hear them praying. All of a sudden, my mentor saw me out of the window, and the Lord spoke to her.

He said, "If you do not get hold of him, he will end up like so many preachers out there, lackadaisical, just doing what he has to in order to get by, satisfied with thinking small and staying small.''

She saw me like that in her mind's eye, and she said, ''That is not the man God is trying to raise up.''

So she ran outside and challenged me.

She said, ''Don't you ever let this happen again. I love you enough to tell you the truth. I know you are mad at me for pushing you to work harder at your calling. But some day you will be glad I cared enough to be this firm with you. You will be glad I love you enough to tell you the truth.''

Today, I understand what she meant, and I love her for encouraging me to think big enough to move out of the small places of ministry.

We need ''coaches'' in the Body of Christ. I want to be one to other people. I want to recognize when I have history in my hands. One of our Olympic stars, Florence Griffith Joyner, tells something that is so important to church leaders.

Before the last Olympics, her coach told her she had ''maxed out.'' He said a runner could only go so fast. She could have believed him and stayed where she was. However, what she did was get another coach, one who believed in her. And she won the gold.

The devil tells you that you have ''maxed out'' as a Christian. You can only go so far, but God says there is no limit to how far you can go. When you became a new creature in Christ (2 Cor. 5:17), you changed coaches. And your new coach says, ''Believe, and all things are possible with Me.'' (Mark 10:27.)

The old coach is jealous and tries to get back in to hinder you and tell you that you have never been anything and never will be. He tells you that you are ugly, silly, and hopeless.

But your new coach tells you that you are the head and not the tail, above and not beneath. (Deut. 28:13.) He tells you that if you keep developing in faith, you will be the person He intended for you to be. Those who walk in the Spirit and not after the flesh are listening to the new coach.

One of the ways I encourage myself is to practice the presence of God. After fighting demons and dealing with people in a service, I will get in a room and say, "Coach, tell me some good things about myself."

And I will hear the Father saying good things to me, encouraging me, and giving me divine ideas. In the middle of a service, I have had the Lord tell me He is proud of me. And I am not special. If you are obedient and faithful to do the things He says, He will be proud of you, too.

I learned a long time ago that God's opinion of me makes man's opinions irrelevant. What counts is what God thinks of us, and He thinks His children are special.

In John 17:22, Jesus said that He wanted to give the disciples the same glory God had given to Him. *Glory* means "to be held in the highest esteem." The Lord holds you in the highest of esteem.

The reason the devil comes after you is because you have everything he wanted. He wanted the glory, and born-again men and women have gotten it, while his destination is outer darkness and the lake of fire. We have gotten the glory because Jesus gave it to us, not because we deserve it.

In addition to needing encouragement to do what God intends for us to do, we need it to keep going following victories. Many times, we go from peak times to weak times. That is one reason you must continually stir up your faith.

There are two times to prepare yourself for an attack of the enemy: when you are really down and when you have had a great victory.

Peak Times to Weak Times

Elijah had the weakest time that is recorded in the Bible right after his greatest victory. He had just challenged the prophets of Baal to a "High Noon" encounter on Mount Carmel — and won. He had walked in the God-kind of faith and caused hundreds of priests of Baal to be killed.

Fire had descended from Heaven and not only consumed the sacrifice to God but the altar *and* all of the water surrounding it in a ditch.

Elijah had faced down hundreds of idolatrous prophets, but then Jezebel threatened him, and he ran. He was under an anointing when he challenged the prophets, but he had to deal with Jezebel as plain old Elijah. So Elijah went from a peak time of pulling on the rope of faith to the next day wanting to die.

He forgot to stir up his faith. Surely, he knew that if God would do what He did at Carmel, He could protect one of his prophets. However, instead of remaining and stirring up his faith, Elijah ran.

Do not ever rest because you are in a peak season and think you are soaring.

Do not quit coming to church, reading the Bible, fasting and praying, and doing the other things that help you soar. Reach out and encourage other people and find someone to encourage you.

People have asked me, "Tim, how come a lot of preachers have fallen right in the middle of their greatest victories, right at the peak of their ministries?"

It is because they let down their guard against the enemy. They think they have it made. They quit stirring all those things inside them that enabled them to get where they are.

One of my friends is also a good friend of Muhammad Ali, the greatest champion boxer of all time. My friend asked Ali what one thing helped him stay on top for so many years, and the champ said that he never stopped working hard at his craft. He never sat down and took victory for granted.

A lot of fighters get great and get lazy. That is what happened to Mike Tyson, when he got beaten by Buster Douglas in Tokyo. That is what caused him to fall into the devil's pitfalls and end up in jail. He started thinking he was so great he was above all ordinary rules and standards.

Certainly I do not approve of what Michael Jackson stands for, but you have to give the guy credit for one thing — he has a strong work ethic. Even though he is on top, he still practices dancing three or four hours a day. When you are on top, you cannot stop, or you will begin to slide backward in any field.

Elijah soared in his personal faith.

He soared in his missions for God.

But he did not know to stir up his faith, and he did not have a Deborah to encourage him.

Some of you may say, "But I don't have a 'significant other' in my life to help me. I do not have a Deborah."

You do have the Holy Spirit, and if you listen to His voice, you will be encouraged. The greatest coach in the universe is the Holy Spirit. He is the main "Coach" of the Trinity. That is one of His roles: to teach and encourage believers.

If you listen carefully for that still, small voice, you can hear Him saying, "Get up. Try it again. You can make it. You can do it one more time. You can glorify the Father."

The Holy Spirit knows He has history in His hands. When you listen to His voice, you are listening to faith, and you will begin to see the potential in yourself and other people and not the problem.

Be willing to go the extra mile, as Deborah was. Bible reference books say that it was five miles from her home on Mount Ephraim to Mount Tabor, where the battle was. That was five hot miles in desert-type country. And she began to speak words of encouragement to him.

She moved Barak from the "Who's He?" into the "Who's Who."

Deborah had a gift of encouragement that only comes from the gift of faith. That is why a lot of people cannot encourage themselves, much less anyone else. They have no faith stirred up in their lives.

She turned Barak's life right side up. True faith always turns your life right side up. Doubt turns it upside down.

Barak was saying, "I don't know if I want to go. These Canaanites are bad news. They don't just kill people, they cut their heads off. They burn people alive. I'm certainly not going without a person of the Living God along!''

One of the things she said to him was: **Is not the Lord gone out before thee?** (Judg. 4:14.)

I have noticed from studying the Bible that when God said He would go out before someone or some people, that usually meant their enemies would be thrown into confusion. The opposing armies would begin to fight one another or run when no one was after them. That is because confusion brings fear, and fear breeds more confusion.

Have you ever noticed that when you are not walking in faith, fear and confusion enter? That is your ''weak time.''

Deborah had history in her hands, and she recognized it.

A man who has influenced me over the years is O. J. Simpson. One day, O. J. walked into an ice cream parlor in San Francisco and saw football star Jim Brown in there buying an ice cream cone.

O. J. walked up to him and said, ''Sir, you are a great running back, and I really admire you.''

Jim Brown said, ''That's great, kid. That's really tremendous.''

And O. J. said, ''I'm going to be a great running back some day. I'm very good now, and one of these days, you never know — I may break some of your records.''

Brown said, ''Hey, boy, that's cute. That's real cute.''

O. J. went on to break almost every one of Jim Brown's records. Little did Brown know that, when he was talking to this young kid, he had history in his hands.

You had better watch how you treat people and be sensitive to the Lord, because you never know when you might have history in your hands. You never know when your encouragement could make or break someone.

When You Have History in Your Hands

An evangelist of the early days of this century named Mordecai Ham once held a revival in a small North Carolina town. Ham was a well-known Messianic Jewish evangelist who did some great exploits, if we had space to tell of them. However, this one night, there were not many people at his meeting.

He could have said, ''This is a dead meeting. Who knows why God sent me here? Maybe I missed it, and I'm tired anyway. We'll just sing a few songs, and I'll say a few words, and go home.''

However, there was a young boy in that meeting named Billy Graham, who got saved that night and grew up to become the greatest evangelist of all time — to date anyway.

When I was in Bible college, I had a lot of big dreams. I would go out onto the beaches outside Miami and witness to the kids. I would hang out on the piers and try to get drug addicts saved.

One of my sisters would say, ''Tim, why don't you give it a rest? You're always into this evangelism.''

But it was like fire in my bones.

One day, I was praying, and I said, ''God, wouldn't it be great if I could win three thousand people to you?''

So I kept witnessing to people, and pretty soon, I felt three thousand was not enough.

Then I said, "What about three million?" And that felt about right.

So I got one of my friends who was an artist to make this sign that said, "Yes, you can: Three Million Souls." I put it over my bed.

When my roommates came in and saw it, they said, "What's Tim up to now? What does that sign mean?"

I said, "That is a goal I have that one day I will have touched three million people for the Lord."

They said, "Oh, come on, Tim. You dream too much."

And they began to tease me about that sign.

If we went to eat in the cafeteria, they would say, "Get out of the way. There are three million souls coming in with Tim."

Or I would be riding in a car with one of them, and I would say, "Be careful," about some traffic situation, and he would say, "I forgot! I have three million people in the car."

Little did they know that they were actually telling the truth. At that time, I was only a young guy with a lot of dreams. But I kept stirring up my faith and that rope got longer. Now I have passed the mark of speaking to three million people.

That happened in about a quarter of the time I thought it would take. Little did my friends know that the goal I set came from God.

So if you are frustrated where you are, I need to tell you this: There always will be problems. First there is the promise, then there are the principles by which you walk out the promise, and finally, there are the problems. No person ever reached his potential without problems. Sometimes not having an encourager is the problem. Sometimes, problems are finances or other circumstances.

Barak's attitude was a problem to Deborah, but she did not let it stop her achieving what God had told her to do. Jezebel was a problem to Elijah, and God Himself became his encourager.

Do not let problems defeat you. Look on them as stepping stones to the next level of faith.

8

Problems Are Part of the Harvest

Problems are not foreign objects in the Christian life. They are part of the harvest. If you do not have problems, you are "dead." Jesus had problems, and we certainly are no better than our Savior. He asked the Father not to take the disciples out of the world but to protect them *in* it. (John 17:15.)

Jesus is our example, and He knew that every problem really is a potential faith-step. The thing that makes the difference is how you handle problems. You need to begin to look on them as challenges, as hurdles to jump over. You need to understand that every problem is a positive possibility.

First the problems, then the breakthrough, the answer, the prosperity. Usually, you do not get to the promise God has given you except through a time of great testing. Look how many years Abraham wandered around the Middle East, dealing with family problems (Lot), wars (Gen. 14), problems in his own character of fear or doubt, and then, finally, God's instruction to offer Isaac as a sacrifice!

Promises, principles, and problems are "seasons" of faith, just as there are steps of faith and levels of faith.

The first thing that happens in the seasons of faith is receiving that promise from God of the miracle you are going to get. Then as you progress through the steps of faith and obedience, that miracle goes into motion.

God said to Elijah, "I am going to send you to a widow, who will feed you." That was the promise.

Then He gave Elijah the principle: "Be obedient and follow my commandments, and you will get to the miracle. Get up and go to Zarephath."

Suppose Elijah thought, "Well, that's not even in Israel. Zarephath is in Sidon. That's where Jezebel is from — Tyre and Sidon. That's "Baal" country. This couldn't be God, or I must have misunderstood. I think perhaps I'll go down to Jerusalem. That's where the temple is. They may not like me in Samaria (capital of Israel), but they will appreciate a man of God in Jerusalem (Judah). Someone there surely will feed me."

What would have happened? If Jezebel had not gotten him, he probably would have starved to death. You only have protection from God when you are following His will and under His wings. If you start off doing your own thing, you are not going to end up with a fulfilled promise. You have just stopped your miracle when you move out of the will of God through disobedience, complacency, or doubt and self-will.

You never get the blessings without the responsibility.

Elijah was responsible to obey God. Not just his own welfare was at stake. There was the widow woman, her son, and her family. Also, God saw far down the years to the time when His Son would be on earth attempting to get His own people to receive Him. And God used this situation of a foreign woman being fed by Israel's prophet to make a point to the Jews:

"If you do not receive My Son — then, just as happened with My prophets — I will send the miracles to those who are not even part of you."

> ...Verily I say unto you, No prophet is accepted in his own country.
>
> But I tell you of a truth, many widows were in Israel in the days of Elias, when the heaven was shut up three years and six months, when great famine was throughout all the land;
>
> But unto none of them was Elias sent, save unto Sarepta (Zarephath), a city of Sidon, unto a woman that was a widow.
>
> Luke 4:24-26

We need to be like Elijah and fulfill the conditions to receive our miracles.

However, we cannot always copy what someone else did to overcome their obstacles or to obtain their miracle. The best thing to "copy" is faith and obedience.

Let me give you an example. When I was at Bible college, some of the best Christian speakers in the nation were brought in to address the students and faculty.

Once Karl Strader, pastor of Carpenter's Home Church in Florida spoke to us. He pastors a church of several thousand in a town with a population of seventy thousand. Then they brought in Dr. Cho, whose church in South Korea at the time was "only" running about a quarter of a million people.

As a young student, I would watch these "giants" of the faith. I would see how dynamic they were, how polished they were at speaking and handling themselves on the platform, and how well they knew the Word of God.

And I would get intimidated. Karl Strader told us how he fasted every Thursday and memorized scriptures. Once, as he preached to us, he began in Hebrews 11 and quoted every verse in the chapter. Then he moved on to Hebrews 12 and quoted the whole chapter. There is such an anointing on his presentation of the Word of God!

Then he jumped to Psalm 145, because it was in the same context. After that, he went to still another chapter. And he gave us chapter after chapter, all by heart. I was just "blown away," as were many of the others.

Instantly, I thought, "I'm going to do that!"

So I began to fast and pray on Thursdays. I might get half through the day and get a stomach ache or a huge headache. Then I would go to the cafeteria and eat — and feel like the biggest loser in the world.

I would think, "I'm never going to be like Karl Strader."

I tried to memorize scriptures. Then I bought "memory cards," and started trying to learn from them. But I could not get four scriptures in a row by memory.

It would have helped so much if someone had told me two things then:

1. "Inch by inch, and precept by precept" is how you move forward in things of God.

2. Another person's miracle is not always yours. Find God's will for you, and you will be able to do it. Do not copy someone else's steps of faith — find your own.

Do Not Try To Copy Someone Else's Miracle

The thing I should have done was to set myself a goal I could reach of so many scriptures to learn over the next three months, rather than trying to memorize whole chapters.

I should have said, "I would like to live a fasted life and know the Word that well" (which is a valid desire), "so I'm going to start out inch by inch. I am going to fast one meal a week for the first three months. Then, when I have done that, it will increase my faith for more."

A lot of people get frustrated, because they "bite off more than they can chew" at one time. They reach beyond where their faith is. If you have a "measure" of faith, you cannot always believe for cancer to be healed. Begin with headaches.

What I did was like a person fifty pounds overweight who hears how someone else lost all that weight in a week. And they set out to do that and cannot make it. Then they get discouraged and quit trying, so they never lose weight. Instead, they keep gaining, and instead of conquering the problem and putting their miracle in motion, the problem becomes a mountain that is more and more difficult to move.

They should have started with trying to lose a pound a week, perhaps, and tried both diet and exercise until they found which would work for them.

If you have problems, welcome to life! The only way to get through problems is to look at them and find a positive possibility in them. You can do this by holding on to the promises you learned while sitting in faith.

Caleb and Joshua are good examples of this. God promised Israel the land, and said they could take it.

Then he gave them the conditions for the miracle to be put in motion: Hear Him and obey His commandments.

So they got to the edge of the Promised Land, and twelve spies were sent forth to take a look at the enemy. Ten of them came back with a negative report.

Caleb and Joshua said, "The land is flowing with milk and honey. It is a good land. There is plenty of grass for our livestock."

But the other ten said, "There are problems over there. In fact, there are big problems — there are giants! And we are like grasshoppers in our own sight. We are food for those giants."

But Caleb and Joshua had an entirely different attitude toward this "problem." They had been sitting in faith, standing in faith, and learning to walk in faith. They knew if God promised it, they could have it. They began to remember all the things God had done for them before. They began to pull on that rope of faith.

They said, "We are well able to take care of those giants. Remember how God delivered us from Pharoah, even sending us away with their wealth? Remember how He provided food and water for us in the desert? If God is for us, who can be against us?"

They realized that the problem could be reversed and develop their faith and their belief in God. They realized the "giants" were not out there but inside — giants like fear, confusion, cowardice, lack of trust in God, and so forth.

Most Christians know the result of this encounter at the edge of the Promised Land. Instead of great exploits accomplished by great faith, there came death to that generation. Their miracle died right there as a result of doubt, unbelief, self-will, and rebellion. And, just as your faith and encouragement affects other people, so do your failures. Caleb and Joshua, as well as all of the children born during the next thirty-eight years, had to endure a wandering, nomadic life in the wilderness.

Some of you reading this book may already be at this place of problems. If not, you can rest assured you will get there. You can choose which way your miracle goes: into motion or into the grave of dead dreams and visions. The only thing that will help you is to stir up your faith, pull on that rope of past blessings from faith, and move out to do whatever God has said to do.

If you will do that, I believe you will find the problems begin to look more like grasshoppers and less like giants. If you move out to meet the giants, God will give you the battle, and you will not "die in the wilderness."

God did not bring them that far to have them fail — yet they did. They failed because of lack of faith in Him, and lack of courage to be obedient even when they had no faith.

God did not bring you this far — from the promise to the problem — to have you fail. He always makes a way out, just as He does for temptations. If you will take one more step and another and another, you will enter into prosperity. *Inch by inch, it is a cinch.*

Remember the seasons of faith. Remember how God brought you through this and through that, and *know* that He can and will do it again, if you keep moving forward. You have seasons to live through. Just do not become weary in well-doing. At the proper time, you are going to reap a harvest if you do not faint.

Also, you need to understand that, just as you cannot copy someone else's path to a miracle, neither do you have the same seasons as others. Some parts of the world are on different seasons, and Christians are all in different seasons of faith. Do not expect yourself to be at the harvest season simply because someone else close to you is there. You may be still in the planting season.

You may be in a drought to learn how to live on less water, while I may be living near a flourishing stream with water to waste. In every season, there are problems and there are positive aspects. Try to find out what is positive about the season you are in.

At this point — when you are in a drought and someone else is flourishing — the enemy can hinder your miracle by running jealousy across your path. If you follow down that "rabbit trail," you will lose your momentum toward your own miracle. You may wander around in the wilderness for a period of time.

Do not lose heart, do not faint, do not become downcast, do not get jealous of others. Your season is coming. Some people for whom God has prosperity will find it a curse instead of a blessing if they do not learn through problems how to handle and appreciate prosperity.

Also, pastors and church workers need to discern the season in which a person is walking. In some seasons, people need help. They need sympathy and attention. They may need to go through other seasons, and if you help them out, God will have to send them back through another season like it in order to make the next step He wants them to make.

A lot of people in an "up" season do not have enough compassion for those who are down. Everyone of us needs to remember what we have walked through to get where we are.

In every one of your problems, or your seasons, there will be a "giant," who says, "Absolutely not! You can't come into the Promised Land."

But one of the best things about Christianity is that, if you keep moving in faith, you become a "giant killer." And once you kill one giant, you know how to kill the next and the next.

David said, "With God's help, I've killed a lion and a bear, and Goliath, you are next!"

We can be like that.

My desire has been to encourage many through this book to become people of great faith. My desire has been to stir up many of those reading this who are young Billy Graham's, or old Elijah's, or timid Deborah's. I do not want to have history in my hands and miss it.

If William J. Seymour with all of his handicaps and problems could be humble and have enough faith in God to be used the way he was — then so can you. I doubt if anyone today has to overcome any worse things than he did. And he overcame them by simply being obedient to God. He did not strive to become great, or even study the great leaders of the past to see how they did it. He simply heard God and had faith to believe and obey.

Any one of us could do that — if we chose.

My prayer is that many will read these words of encouragement and rise up to become those who change their worlds and do great exploits with God.

Notes

Notes

Notes

Notes

Notes

Notes

Notes

Notes

Notes